THE CLOUD OF UNKNOWING

THE CLOUD OF UNKNOWING

a new paraphrase

by

Halcyon Backhouse

Backhouse, Halcyon
The Cloud of unknowing: a new paraphrase.
1. Cloud of unknowing (paraphrase)
I. Title
248.4 BV5082

ISBN 0-340-36868-x

Paraphrase copyright © 1985 by Robert Backhouse. First published 1985. All rights reserved. No part of this publication may be reproduced, stored in a retrieval system, or transmitted, in any form or by any means, electronic, mechanical, photocopying, recording or otherwise, without the prior permission of the publishers. Printed in Great Britain for Hodder and Stoughton, Editorial Office: 47 Bedford Square, London WC1 3DP by Richard Clay (The Chaucer Press) Ltd, Bungay, Suffolk.

HODDER AND STOUGHTON
LONDON SYDNEY AUCKLAND TORONTO

British Library Cataloguing in Publication Data

Backhouse, Halcyon
    The cloud of unknowing: a new paraphrase. –
    (Hodder Christian paperbacks)
    1. Christian life
    I. Title
    248.4   BV4501.2

    ISBN 0–340–36868–3

Contents

8

Foreword

We live in an age of activism. Everywhere there is concern to improve the world – or at least to change it. Christians of all traditions are placing more emphasis on social concern and political involvement. With the Lausanne Congress in 1974 the worldwide evangelical movement acknowledged with penitence its neglect of social concern and resolved to put matters right. Billy Graham, while remaining firmly committed to the gospel of personal conversion, has begun also to stress that Christian commitment involves social concern. All of this is good and proper, but it is not without its dangers. If our action in the world is to be of lasting spiritual value it is essential that it should have deep Christian roots. This means, among other things, that it is important to preserve and to nurture an inner relationship with God in Jesus Christ, a deep spiritual life. Otherwise our outward acts are liable to dissolve into a merely secular activism.

It is appropriate that at this time there is a rekindling of interest in the spiritual classics of the past. More than one series of religious books have recently appeared: the *Classics of Western Spirituality* (SPCK), the *Classics of Faith and Devotion* (Pickering and Inglis) and now the *Hodder Christian Classics*. These and other recent volumes on the subject are very welcome. In particular, the present series offers more than simply literal translations. The aim is to 'retell' the works of the past for today, keeping close to the original meaning but expressing it in terms which relate to us today. This approach is welcome in that it makes the great classics of the past accessible to many who would not persevere with a more literal translation.

But why should we read books from the past, anyway? Is it not safer and easier to keep to the latest modern paperbacks? Easier maybe, but certainly not safer or more worthwhile. C. S. Lewis answered this question well in his essay 'On the Reading of Old Books'.[1]

Every age has its own outlook. It is specially good at seeing certain truths and specially liable to make certain mistakes. We all, therefore, need the books that will correct the characteristic mistakes of our own period. And that means the old books . . .

We may be sure that the characteristic blindness of the twentieth century – the blindness about which posterity will ask, 'But how *could* they have thought that?' – lies where we have never suspected it, and concerns something about which there is untroubled agreement between Hitler and President Roosevelt or between Mr H. G. Wells and Karl Barth. None of us can fully escape this blindness, but we shall certainly increase it, and weaken our guard against it, if we read only modern books. Where they are true they will give us truths which we half knew already. Where they are false they will aggravate the error with which we are already dangerously ill. The only palliative is to keep the clean sea breeze of the centuries blowing through our minds, and this can be done only by reading old books. Not, of course, that there is any magic about the past. People were no cleverer than they are now; they made as many mistakes as we. But not the *same* mistakes. They will not flatter us in the errors we are already committing; and their own errors, being now open and palpable, will not endanger us. Two heads are better than

[1] C. S. Lewis, *Undeceptions* (London, Geoffrey Bles, 1971), pp. 162 ff.

one, not because either is infallible, but because they are unlikely to go wrong in the same direction.

No one generation has all the answers. When it comes to nuclear physics, we may well know more than our ancestors; when it comes to spirituality, the roles are reversed. By opening ourselves to the heritage of the past we gain access to a wealth of spiritual wisdom.

But why should we read books from other traditions? Why should a Protestant want to read the writings of a Catholic mystic? A simple glance at a hymn book will show that many who disagree radically over doctrine are able to sing one another's hymns with enthusiasm. Christians are less divided in their worship and in their spiritual lives than in their beliefs. Furthermore, as the blind spots of our generation can be exposed by the past, so can the blind spots of our tradition be exposed by the spiritual writings of another tradition. In particular, the Reformation swept away much medieval corruption (such as veneration of saints and relics) but also much positive spirituality. The Protestant spiritual tradition has often been the poorer for it. For instance, modern evangelical teaching on prayer is often very superficial and there is little incentive to progress beyond the most basic levels. Just as Roman Catholics today are learning from Protestant traditions of extempore prayer, so Protestants today can learn from the Catholic tradition. The medieval Catholic mystics, like the anonymous author of *The Cloud of Unknowing*, can assist us in deepening our prayer lives. If read slowly, meditatively and with discernment, classics like the present volume can be a great stimulus to our spiritual lives.

A. N. S. Lane MA BD
Lecturer in Historical
Theology at the
London Bible College

Translator's preface

Few contemporary Christian books are apt for the spirit of this age. Even fewer meet this age with a thrill, compulsion and mysterious dynamism that holds the reader spellbound to the very last word. Yet the *Cloud of Unknowing*'s author still achieves this 500 years after he first wrote this book.

It is generally accepted that the same unknown medieval author penned certainly four, possibly seven, Middle-English prose treatises: *The Cloud of Unknowing*, *The Book of Privy Counselling*, *The Epistle of Prayer*, *The Epistle of Discretion in Stirrings*, and also *Of Discerning Spirits*, *Denis Hid Divinity*, and *Benjamin Minor*.

The Cloud is the earliest of these extant works. Its subject-matter deals with the highest form of contemplative prayer. The author discusses the being of God. He emphasises that this united prayer of the will is the highest act, superior to reason, reaching its object, God, where reason fails.

Yet this most marvellous account of true spirituality was never intended for publication. The receiver of the original manuscript was under strict instruction not to let the contents become public. Have we violated his bid for secrecy? Yet dare we not make its contents public? Whoever reads this must be inspired by a new understanding of the spiritual paths of men and women who walk with God.

This retelling has attempted to be true to the original intention and spirit of the author. It is not a comprehensive or definitive rendering of the original. Some paragraphs have had to be reorganised and some sentences reshaped in order to facilitate a smoother rendering. Middle English has a beauty that is not easily transposed into today's language, but in trying to make this book available to a wider audience, I have tried to retain something of its innate poetry. So here, hopefully, is a fresh, clear, uncluttered, dynamically equivalent paraphrase of *The Cloud of Unknowing*.

The author

Father Baker's commentary on *The Cloud of Unknowing* (p. 289) and Dom. Knowles's *The English Mystics* (p.90) both suggest that the author deliberately took pains to remain unknown. Despite much discussion on the question of the identity of the author, the problem has remained unsolved.

He is strikingly individual in his teaching. But he probably was a priest, for he gives his blessing at the end of three of his treatises, and he is careful to insist that the dogma and traditional practices of the Church must be understood as the basics of mystical prayer. He was a contemplative and was obviously recognised as a director of souls, for he habitually instructs young disciples in their spiritual exercises with the voice of authority. It is generally agreed that the author had retired from a monastery to the greater seclusion of a hermitage.

The date and place

Dr Hodgson's edition of the Middle-English text suggests that there is little evidence in determining the exact date of *The Cloud*, but that it was likely to have been written in the late fourteenth century – Chaucer's century. The language tends to support the theory that the manuscript was written in the central district of the North-East Midlands. There are seventeen different texts of *The Cloud of Unknowing* and they have been fully discussed in Dr Phyllis Hodgson's scholarly edition of the Middle-English text.[1] Indeed, anyone wishing to study this book from a complete and scientific viewpoint would be obliged to refer to her edition of manuscript. But the reader not conversant with Middle English would find this difficult.

The setting

The fourteenth century was marked by an almost continual round of wars in England. Edward III (1327–1377) carried on a non-stop battle with France, and the Scots were embroiled with England in the early half of the century, while popular insurrection manifested itself because of social distress in the last quarter of the century. The Church was not much better off than the State: the former's authority was weakened and impaired by the great schism of the West (1378), and the Great Plague in the middle of the century had done immeasurable harm to the clergy by destroying so many of them. By the end of the century, the Lollard movement rose in alliance with the anti-clerical nobility and John Wycliffe, its chief preacher, had begun to agitate within the Church.

Altogether it was an era of stress. Yet England produced four of the greatest mystics of that century – the author of *The Cloud*, Richard Rolle, Walter Hilton and Julian of Norwich. In *The Cloud* we have evidence that it was possible for a man to possess his soul in peace despite the external violence and distress of his age.

About the book

The Cloud of Unknowing is the work of a man of great spiritual gifts. Not only does he display a mind and heart sublimely

[1] Dr Phyllis Hodgson, *The Cloud of Unknowing* (Oxford University Press, 1944)

attractive to others, but he possesses the capacity to attract others by powerful expression. The original work moves slowly yet with tremendous inner activity: profound thought and literary beauty is instinctively delivered with contagious enthusiasm. Yet it is a difficult book. For mysticism is more than doctrine: it is life. It is not a philosophical theory or vague feeling of literary pleasure. It is a practical thing engulfing the personality. *The Cloud* is a muezzin-like call to all Christians for a most carefully defined and exacting life of the spirit; yet it is a call to only the few who, by grace and disposition, can respond to it.

The author emphasises the antithesis of reason and will, of knowing and loving. He teaches his disciples to renounce discursive thought, to simplify the intellectual act, and above all to love. For 'love may reach God in this life, but not knowing.' At the height of his effort to love God the contemplative is face to face with a dark cloud of unknowing. To love God is the whole exercise of his will. The point is single, not several, and the author is at pains to make it clear: to possess God in this life is all one needs; it is the beginning of the life of heaven.

The Divine Cloud of Unknowing[1]

HERE BYGYNND A BOOK OF CONTEMPLATION OF WHICHE IS CLEPYD DE CLOWDE OF YNKNOWYNG, IN DE WHICHE A SOULE IS ONYD WID GOD

---

[1]This title occurs in some fifteenth-century manuscripts, and it was under this that the book, edited by H. Collins (London, 1871), was first printed by Father Augustine Baker.

Prayer

God,
To whom all hearts are open,
to whom all wills speak
and from whom no secret is hid,
I beg you
so to cleanse the intent of my heart
with the unutterable gift of your grace
that I may perfectly love you
and worthily praise you. Amen.

Prologue

In the name of the Father, and of the Son and of the Holy Ghost.

Whoever you are, and however you got hold of this book, whether you own it, keep it, carry it or are borrowing it — you're the one I'm speaking to.

I charge you, and I beg you, with all the strength and power for good which God's love gives me: don't talk about this book to anyone. Don't let anyone read it, or write about it, or speak about it, unless in your opinion that person is truly and totally determined to be a perfect follower of Christ. And I don't mean just an activist. I mean a follower in the deepest sense, someone who wants to live a life of contemplation because this is the way, even in this life and though we are only human, to become perfect by God's grace. Give this book only to someone whose way of living has for some time shown you that he has what it takes to enter the contemplative life. Otherwise none of this will be of any value to him.

On top of this, I give you a further charge, by the authority of love itself: pass on to whoever does read, write, speak or hear of this book, what I am about to entrust to you, urging that they take time over it. It could be that the content in the beginning or middle is not altogether clear and is only fully explained at the end. If someone merely looked at part of the book he could quite easily be led astray. So, to avoid this error, I beg you, or anyone else, for love's sake, do as I ask.

But as for idle-chatterers, flatterers, self-denigrators, fault-finders, gossips, whisperers, tell-tales, and grumblers of every type, well I couldn't care one bit if they never see this book. I did not write it for them. In fact, I'd prefer it if they steered clear of it; they and all the intellectuals or the merely curious. They may well be good men from the 'active' point of view, but this book will be meaningless to them. Only those who, though they may appear active, are also stirred within by the inner working of God's Spirit (and his judgments are hidden to us), lean towards the contemplative life. Not continually, perhaps, as is the way with true contemplatives, but certainly they will occasionally share in the highest levels of the act of contemplation. They are the ones who, if by God's grace they see this book, will discover its comfort.

There are seventy-five chapters on this subject, and the last five show how you may know for certain whether God has called you to this work or not.

A brief address to the reader

My friend in God,
I sincerely beg you to consider carefully your calling and how you should achieve it. Thank God from the bottom of your heart that by his grace you may bear up in the state, stage and way of life that you have wholeheartedly entered upon. And that you may win through to the crown of everlasting life in spite of all the deceits and attacks of your physical and spiritual enemies.

1 Four stages of Christian life

Spiritual friend in God, it strikes me, in my own rough and ready way, that there are four stages or kinds of Christian life: common, special, solitary and perfect. The first three begin and end in this life; the fourth, may begin here, solely by God's grace, but it is never-ending, continuing on into heaven! You'll notice that they are in sequence and it is in this same order that our Lord in his great mercy has called you, leading you on to himself by your own inward desire.

You know perfectly well how God led you through his everlasting love when you were in the common stage of your Christian life. That same love which created you out of nothing, then brought you back when you, through Adam's nature, were lost to him, that love compelled you in the first place to turn away from the kind of life that was so far from him. Having lit the flame of your own love, he then graciously fanned its flames so that you were bound to him and so he led you on to the more special life as a servant among his other servants. All this he accomplished for the sole purpose of enabling you to grow spiritually, on a deeper level than in the common state of Christian living.

But there's even more: God was not content to leave you at that stage, either. Given the nature of the love he has always had for you, he has in his own delightful way drawn you to a yet further stage, still closer to himself. By his grace you became solitary, committed to him and desiring none other than himself. This is where you now are and from where you will learn to take the first loving steps to the life of perfection, the final stage in your relationship with God.

2 Lay hold of God

First, go, take stock of who you are. Pause for thought and realise that even now you are no more than a wretched weakling. Who are you and what have you done to deserve this high calling from our Lord? God's love invites and attracts you to live a life completely in him and your soul hesitates in its response: how sluggish, how slothful!

Right now, wretched fellow, keep an eye on your enemy, your self. Don't fall into the trap of pride, thinking yourself better than everyone because you live the solitary life and are being called to higher things. Quite the opposite: unless you heed your calling, helped as you are by God's grace and direction, you are even more pitiable and wretched than everyone else. This should be the point where you are: even more humble and loving to your spiritual husband who is none other than Almighty God himself. This King of kings and Lord of lords has in humility stepped down to your level. He has graciously chosen you out of his flock to be his very special one. You are to feed on the sweet food of God's love and dwell in his rich pastures, delighting in a foretaste of the kingdom of heaven which is your inheritance.

So, I beg you, go on quickly. Look ahead, not behind. See where you are missing out and don't be content with what you already possess of God's love. As you know more of God, your knowledge will prove the quickest way to true humility. Your whole life must be constrained by a longing for God if you are to achieve perfection. This longing will arise from your innermost being, brought to life by God and freely accepted by you. But be warned: he is a jealous lover and will tolerate no rival. He asks for nothing else than you alone. His will is that you should look to him and let him have his way. It is therefore important that your spiritual windows and doorways be firmly guarded against enemy attacks. If you are willing to do this, you need only to lay hold upon God humbly in prayer and he will come to you.

Lay hold of him, then, and see how things go. God is waiting for you and ever ready to be with you. 'But how and what do I do,' you ask, 'if I am to lay hold of God?'

3 Faith and grace

Lift up your heart to God. In humble and total love for him seek God himself. Do not consider what the rewards may be. Refuse utterly to think of anything that detracts from God himself. Forget the world and everything in it, forget your own understanding of its meaning, so that your singleness of mind may not be distracted from God himself. Let go! Give yourself over entirely to God's pleasure. Saints and angels rejoice when you do this and hasten to help you forward. The evil ones are furious, however, and will try in every way to deflect you. But the whole of mankind, in a most mysterious and wonderful way, will be helped by your action. Indeed, the very souls in purgatory will find their pain eased by the goodness of your actions. And you yourself can discover no better way to be purified than by seeking that to which you are called: knowing God. Your soul will be helped by God's grace when it consciously longs to be in union with God. And it can happen in no time at all, in a flash, in a moment. If it did not, the struggle would be too hard and beyond your powers. So press on. Don't give up. Work away at it until this longing to know God surges up within you.

When you first begin, you may find only darkness – a cloud of unknowing, as it were. It will seem incomprehensible, meaningless, except that in your innermost will you will feel a simple steadfast intention reaching out towards God. No matter what you do, this darkness, this cloud, will seem to remain between you and God. It will stop you seeing God in the clear light of rational understanding and from experiencing his loving mercy in your inner being. But be reconciled to the fact that you must wait in this darkness as long as necessary, and don't give up. Continue to struggle, longing to know God whom you love. For if you are ever to feel him and see him in this life, it will always be in this darkness, this cloud. But if you work hard at what I tell you, I believe you will arrive there. Through God's mercy you will achieve your heart's desire.

4 Without knowledge or imagination

But so that you don't go wrong in this and make mistakes, let me tell you a bit more about the way I see things.

This work of contemplation does not take a long time to accomplish. It is the shortest work one can imagine. It is no more or less than an atom, the smallest particle of time known to philosophers of astronomy. In fact, it is so tiny that it is beyond analysis, beyond understanding. Long ago it was said of these same moments of time: 'All the time that is given to thee, it shall be asked of thee, how thou hast spent it.' And quite right, too. We should be asked to give an account of time, of how we respond to each single precise stirring of God within a will at the centre of the soul.

As many atoms in time move within that hour, so do such impulses of the will. Had you by grace been restored to the state of innocence before Man's Fall, then you would, by that same grace, be in control of those inner stirrings. Then no one would go astray, but we would all reach for the sovereign desire, for the highest will, for God himself.

For he condescends to meet us with his Godhead at the level we can grasp. So the soul can commune with God, because it is created in his image and likeness. It is God alone who can utterly satisfy the soul, completely and totally fulfilling the soul's will and desire. The soul, restored by grace, is in love, perfectly able to understand the things of

God, though these things are quite incomprehensible to the natural intelligence of both man and angel. Even angels, after all, are no more than created beings. What I am saying is this: love succeeds where intellect fails.

All rational creatures, angels and men, possess two distinct powers: that of knowing and that of loving. To the first, the creator God is forever incomprehensible. But to the second, to the power of love, God is totally knowable. Any single loving soul may know for himself the God who is incomparably sufficient to fill all the souls and angels that exist. This is the marvellous miracle of love. Flowering ceaselessly, it is the work of the eternal God. Those who by grace know this for themselves live in endless bliss; but its opposite is endless pain.

If anyone were so transformed by God's grace that he could respond to every stirring of his will, then he would never be without a taste of that eternal sweetness. Yes, even here in this life, he would know something of the bliss of heaven though without the full joy.

So, do not be surprised that I spur you on. It is what man would be engaged in today (as you will hear later) had he not sinned. This is what man was created for. Everything else was made to enable him to achieve it. This is how man will be made whole again. When this work of contemplation is neglected, a man falls deeper and deeper into sin, alienated and estranged from God. But if it is obeyed and worked at attentively, a man rises above sin, drawing evermore close to God.

So be very conscious of time. There is nothing more precious. In a moment heaven may be won or lost. It shows how valuable time is, for God, the giver of time, never presents two separate moments at once but always one after the other. Otherwise he would have to reverse the order and course of creation.

Time is made for man, not man for time. God, who rules nature, made time for man, and man's inner impulses moment by moment are in harmony with the flow of time. God will not obstruct this. So, on Judgment Day, man won't be able to excuse himself by pointing the finger at God. When he has to give an account of how he has spent his time he won't be able to say: 'God, you gave two moments at the same time and I had only one moment of impulse!'

You may now be saying sadly, 'What shall I do? If what you say is true how am I going to account for my moments? Here am I, twenty-four years old, and up to now I've been blind to the importance of time. It's clear, from what you've already written, that I can't redeem that wasted time – it's not possible, neither in my own strength, nor God's. Even if I were to mend my ways there is no extra time to cover the past – only future time to work on. Furthermore, I know only too well from personal experience that I shall still only be able to respond to one in a hundred future impulses! Weak-witted and stupid as I am, I'm really cornered! Help me, now, for the love of Jesus!'

How right you are to say 'for the love of Jesus'. For it is in the love of Jesus that you shall find help. Love has, by its very nature, the power to share in all things. So love Jesus, and all that is his will be yours. He makes and gives time because he is God. And because he is Man, he is the true controller. So by virtue of both his Godhead and Manhood, Jesus is the ultimate judge to whom you must give an account of your time. Unite with him in love and faith. Then in that bond you will be joined not only to him but to all who, like yourself, are in union with him in love. That includes Mary, Jesus's mother, who, full of grace, perfectly heeded every moment. It includes all the angels of heaven who have never let time lazily slip past, and all the saints on earth and in heaven, who, through grace, took careful note of time because of their love for God.

Look, there is comfort here! Be wise, understand, and gain from it. But let me underline what I've said: I cannot envisage anyone claiming true fellowship in this way with Jesus, or his mother, his high angels or his saints, who is not doing everything in his power, by the help of grace, to make the most of time. He must be seen to be able to help the fellowship in whatever little way he can.

So, pay the utmost attention to his acts and to the marvellous work of grace within your soul. It always stirs suddenly, unexpectedly, rapidly springing up to God like sparks from the coal. It is incredible how many times such impulses may rise in just a single hour in the soul set to this work. In a flash, the soul completely forgets the world around. Yet as quickly as the impulse comes, so it goes. Man's fallen nature once more relapses into worldly thoughts, preoccupied with memories of deeds done or not done. But don't worry. As fast again it will arise, and as suddenly as it always does.

This, briefly, is how it works and you may be quite sure that it is far from fantasy, weird imaginings or ingenious speculation. They stem from pride, curiosity and clever inventiveness, not from the simple, devout yet blind stirring of love. The proud, curious mind must always be harshly trodden under foot, if this work is to be truly begun in purity of spirit. For anyone hearing or reading about this who thinks that the knowledge of God is something that can be gained by intellectual activity has completely misunderstood the whole thing. He will conjure up images and display experiences which are not of the physical world or of the spiritual world. Such a man is dangerously deceived. Indeed, unless God in his great goodness and mercy miraculously causes him to change direction, and leads him to experienced workers who can counsel him, the man will go mad. Or else he will fall into some other kind of spiritual mischief and devil's deceit. At the end of it he may be lost eternally in body and soul. So, for the love of God, be extremely careful never to embark upon the work of contemplation as an intellectual experience. I tell you the truth: it cannot come that way, so leave it alone.

Don't think that because I call it a 'darkness' or a 'cloud' that it is what you see in the sky or the kind of darkness you get indoors when the lights are out. That kind of darkness and cloud you may picture with your imagination whether in the height of summer or the depth of winter. That is not at all what I mean. By 'darkness' I mean a lack of 'knowing' just as all things that you do not know or have forgotten are 'dark' to you, for you cannot see it with your spiritual eye. For this reason it is called not a cloud of the sky but a 'cloud of unknowing'. It remains between you and your God.

5   Hidden under the cloud of forgetting

If you ever come to this cloud to live and work in it, this is what you must do: just as the 'cloud of unknowing' is above you, between you and God, so you must put a 'cloud of forgetting' below you, between you and all creation. Perhaps you think that you will be far away from God, with this cloud between you, but surely it follows that you are further away than ever if there is no cloud of forgetting between you and 'all creatures'? By 'all creatures' I mean not only the creatures themselves but everything connected with them, including physical and spiritual beings, irrespective of their state or of how good or evil they are. Everything, without exception, must be removed, hidden under the cloud of forgetting.

At other times it may well be valuable to think of certain people – who they are and what they do – but in this case it is of little value, if any. For calling to mind an individual affects the spirit. Your soul's eye focuses on him just as a marksman fixes his eyes on his target. I can tell you that everything you thus engage your mind in comes between you and God, with the result that you become further away from him. Nothing but God must fill your mind.

In fact, if I may say so with all due reverence, when we are doing this work it is of little value even to dwell on God's kindness or worthiness, or on Mary, the saints or angels, or on the joys of heaven itself. It is no use thinking that such meditation will strengthen your purpose. I can tell you that it will not help one whit. For although it may usually be good to think of God's kindness and to love him and praise him for it, it is far better to contemplate God as he is, and to love him and praise him for himself alone.

6   A question raised about this book

Well now, naturally you may well ask: 'How am I to think of God himself? And what is he?' The only answer I can give is: 'I don't know!'

Your question once again draws me into that same darkness, that same cloud of unknowing in which I want you to be! For though we can, through grace, know and think about the workings of most matters, and even those of God, yet of God himself no man can think. Consequently, I would set aside everything that can be thought about and choose for my love God – whom I cannot think about! Why? For the very fact that he can be loved and not reasoned. By love he may be sought and held, but not by thought. So, although it may be good at times to consider the kindness and worthiness of God, and though it may be enlightening and part of contemplation, nevertheless, in this work, it should be cast aside and covered with a cloud of forgetting. Step on it resolutely and enthusiastically with a devout and kindling love, and try to penetrate that darkness above you. Strike hard at that thick cloud of unknowing with a sharp dart of longing love. And whatever happens, don't give up.

7 Dealing with one's thoughts

If thoughts arise and press down between you and that darkness, questioning you: 'What do you seek? What do you want?', reply: 'I want God. I covet him. I seek him. I want nothing but him.'

And should reason persist: 'What is that God?', then say, 'It is the God who made me and redeemed me, and who has graciously called me to his love. You have no place here, for thought cannot begin to know him, so get down!' Then tread heavily upon your thought, pushing it down, out of love for God. Do this even if it appears to you to be most holy and reasonable and would help you find God.

It is possible that thought will bring to mind many beautiful, wonderful aspects of God's kindness, reminding you of his sweetness, love, grace and mercy. If you listen to it, he will ask no more, chattering on incessantly until you slowly come down to think of Christ's passion. There thought will show you the wonderful kindness of God and he wants nothing better than that you listen to him. Soon he will show you your old wretched life, and as you dwell on it you will be carried away into its past haunts and associations. Before you know it, you're all over the place! The reason why you lost your single-mindedness was because you chose to listen to that thought, then engaged it, and so got carried away by it.

'Yet, what thought communicated was both good and holy, even necessary: no one can possibly do the work of contemplation without having first been able to meditate on his own sinfulness, the Lord's passion, God's kindness and great goodness and worth. Otherwise surely he would go wrong in contemplation, coming to a halt altogether? But yet, whoever has practised meditation must nevertheless leave it alone. He must submerge meditation under the cloud of forgetting if he is ever to pierce that cloud of unknowing between himself and his God.

So when you have set yourself to this work, when you feel that God in his grace has called you to it, lift up your heart to him in humble love: it is God who created you, redeemed you and by grace called you to this work. Let this be your only thought of God, nothing else, for it is your desire that matters. A naked intent directed to God, without any other desire than him alone, is all that is required.

And if you want to sum up just what this intent is, and to remember it more easily, then choose any small word of one syllable (the shorter the better) which harmonises with the Spirit's work. For example 'God' or 'Love', or whatever suits you best – but make sure it is of one syllable. Then cling on to it so that it is fixed forever within you, come what may.

This word will be both your shield and spear, in peace and in war. With it you will hammer the cloud and this darkness above you. With it you will push down all thought under the cloud of forgetting. If any thoughts try to engage your mind, respond with that one word. And if thought with its great learning seeks to analyse and examine this word, say that you prefer it whole, and refuse to let the word be broken down! If you do this unfailingly, thought will not stay. Why? Because you have not let it feed on other thoughts in helpful meditations, as we've already said.

8 Questions on intelligence, activity and contemplation

Well, now you may ask: 'What is it that tries to intrude into this work of contemplation? Is it good or evil? And if it is evil how amazing that it should help my meditation so much! Indeed, sometimes listening to this is most uplifting. I am even brought to tears when I think of Christ's passion, my sinfulness and so on, so that I'm convinced it must be truly holy and good for me. And if it is good, I'm amazed that you tell me to leave it alone and conceal it under the cloud of forgetting!'

Now this is a good question. I'll try to answer it as best I can. Firstly, when you asked what it was that intrudes into this work and appears to be so helpful, I'd say it is quite clearly a thought of your natural mind, the reasoning part of your soul. And when you ask me whether it is good or evil, I'd say that in essence it must be good for it is a ray of Godlike light. The good or evil lies in how you use this thought. Of course it is good when by grace you see your sinfulness, Christ's passion, his kindness, and God's physical and spiritual creation.

Then it isn't surprising that it should, as you suggest, encourage devotion. But reason becomes evil when it is swollen by pride or is inflamed by mere curiosity and the desire to acquire learning and book-knowledge (as in some of the clergy!). It makes them keen to be well-known. They are no longer humble scholars and masters of divine knowledge, but men with proud devilish intellects, and masters of emptiness, vanity and lies. In everyone, whether they are religious or not, ordinary reason becomes evil when it makes them proud of their worldly success; when they covet worldly honour, position, riches, empty delights, recognition and popularity.

You may well ask me why you should submerge all this in the cloud of forgetting, if it is essentially good and if, when used well, it strengthens your devotions. My answer would be to point out that there are two ways of living the Christian life: one is the active life and the other the contemplative. The active life has a higher and lower life, and the contemplative a lower and higher. They are both so linked that, although different, yet they are interdependent. The higher part of the active life has its counterpart in the lower part of the contemplative life. Thus a man who is fully active must have some of the contemplative in him, and the fully contemplative (on earth, that is) must also be in part active.

The active life is such that it begins and ends here on earth. This is not so of the contemplative life: begun here on earth, it continues into eternity. The part that Mary chose shall never be taken away. The active life is 'troubled and worried' about many things. Contemplatives, however, 'sit in peace with but one thing'.

The lower part of the active life consists of good, honest, wholesome acts of mercy and charity. The higher part of the active life (and the lower part of the contemplative life) is formed of spiritual meditation. You are aware of being self-centred; there is sorrow and confession. You consider Christ's passion, and his servants, you praise God for his wonderful gifts, his kindness and his works in creation, both physical and spiritual. But the higher part of contemplation (as we know it on earth) is shrouded in darkness and in this cloud of unknowing. There, in great love and blind outreach, the soul seeks for the naked being of God alone.

In the lower part of the active life a man lives by exterior things, and they are inferior, beneath him, as it were. In the higher part of the active life (and in the lower part of the contemplative life) a man's life is interior, within himself, and balanced. But in the higher part of the contemplative life a man rises above himself and is subordinate to God alone. He rises above himself, indeed, because, cast upon God's grace, he deliberately seeks to win what is out of his natural reach: to be united with God in spirit, one in love and will.

Just as it is impossible to arrive at the higher part of the active life without letting go of the lower part, so it is impossible to enter the higher part of the contemplative life without relinquishing the lower part. It would be wrong and positively harmful for a man deep in meditation to have to set to and think about practical works – what he has done or should do – even though they are good in themselves. So surely it must be just as wrong and unhelpful for a man in this darkness of the cloud of unknowing, moving in love to God himself, to let any thought or meditation of God's wonderful gifts, kindness and works of creation, physical or spiritual, come between him and his God, no matter how holy or inspiring they may be!

That is why I ask you to suppress such sharp, subtle thought. Cover it with a thick cloud of forgetting; yes, even when it is holy and well-intentioned. It is love alone that can reach God himself in this life, and not knowledge. While the soul lives in this perishable body, its spiritual understanding, especially of God, is somehow distorted. One's work, therefore, becomes imperfect and, if it wasn't for God's grace, would lead us into a number of errors.

9 In contemplation thoughts hinder, rather than help

So, the vigorous working of your understanding, which is always trying to take over when you are engaged in this blind work, must be held down. Unless you suppress it, it will suppress you! Just when you think that you are living in this darkness and that nothing but God fills your mind, on closer inspection you find that your mind is caught up with something quite definitely less than God! When that happens, this thing is on top of you, between you and your God.

Decide, then, to push down all such thoughts, however attractive or holy they may be. I can quite confidently tell you one thing: it is more profitable to your soul, more innately worthwhile, and more pleasing to God, to all saints and angels in heaven (yes, and more helpful to your spiritual and natural friends, alive or dead), that you should have this blind longing for the love of God himself, than that you pursue thoughts of God. It is better that your secret love should press upon this 'cloud of unknowing', that this should be your deep spiritual desire, than that you gaze on the angels and saints in heaven, or hear their happy music in bliss.

Don't be surprised at this. If you could see him once (as you can by grace), and touch him and feel him in this life, then you would agree with me. But be quite sure that you shall never see God clearly in this life; but, by his grace, you may feel his presence if it is his will. So lift up your love to that cloud – or rather, as I should really say, let God draw your love up to that cloud. Strive, with the help of his grace, to forget all else.

If a random involuntary thought can move you away from God, can hinder you, and stop you exploring his love, how much more will a deliberate thought deflect your purpose? And if it is true that your progress is impeded when you think about special saints or spiritual matters, how much more will you be hindered when you think about ordinary people belonging to this wretched life?

I'm not saying that a spontaneous thought about a good and spiritual thing is evil. Neither is a deliberate thought about, for example, how to deepen your devotion. No! God forbid that you should think I mean this. What I do say is that even though such thoughts are good and holy, in this particular case they hinder more than they help. For surely, anyone seeking God perfectly will not be content to rest in thoughts of angels or heavenly saints.

10 When a thought is deadly sin

A sudden thought springing spontaneously to mind and demanding your attention cannot be imputed to you as sin. It is the result of original sin and you were cleansed from the guilt of that sin at baptism.

But if you do not quickly overcome this sudden impulse, whether it is pleasing or distressing, then it can take hold of your mind and become sin. If someone who is living in unredeemed sin allows such a thought to dominate his thinking, then it is a mortal sin. But, for you, and anyone else who has truly forsaken the world to become a sincere and obedient member of the Church, no longer trying to please himself but serving others, such thoughts are not grave sins, but venial. This is because you have set your heart on God, you are rooted and grounded in him, and you are led by him as by a loving father.

But give all those thoughts houseroom instead of marching orders, and they will in the end take root in your inmost soul, at the centre of your will, becoming deadly sin. And this can happen when you, or anyone else, purposely draws upon memories of people or things. So if, for instance, something has upset you, and you start to feel very strongly about it, and want to get your own back – this is then anger. Or else something happens which you hate and condemn – that could be envy. Or perhaps you begin to get tired and bored with the fight to be good in body and spirit – that is sloth.

And, there again, if it is a pleasant thought, and you experience a fleeting delight whenever it recurs, then you will want to stay with it! In the end your heart and mind will constantly return to it, feeding on it. You will want nothing more than to live undisturbed with this pleasant feeling. If this thought is deliberately recalled or welcomed when it comes, and it causes you to dwell on your own worth or knowledge, on how charming you are, or how important, well-favoured or beautiful – then it is pride.

If the thought is about goods and chattels, riches, possessions and ownership – then it is covetousness. If it is about fancy food which delights the taste-buds – then it is gluttony. If it is full of love or desire and any form of physical indulgence, flirting, flattering yourself or someone else – then it is lust.

11 Evaluate each thought and impulse

I'm not saying this because I believe that you, or anyone else I have mentioned, are guilty and weighed down by these sins but because I want you to carefully evaluate each thought and impulse. I want you to be able to destroy it the instant it appears and presents you with the opportunity to sin. I can tell you this for sure: anyone who sets little store by that first, apparently innocent, thought, and doesn't weigh up its implications, will not be able to stop himself from carelessly slipping into venial sin. Such sin which is not serious, cannot be totally avoided in this life. But all true disciples striving for perfection should shun it from their lives, or else it should come as no surprise that it soon turn into deadly sin!

12 Sin destroyed, virtue born

So, therefore, never give up your resolve, but beat away at this cloud of unknowing between you and God with that sharp dart of longing love. Dislike intensely all thoughts other than those of God himself. Let nothing put you off. It is the only way that you can destroy the very ground and root of sin. No amount of fasting, keeping watch, early rising, sleeping on bare boards, or self-flagellation, is of any use; nor is plucking out your eyes, cutting out your tongue, blocking your ears and nose, amputating your limbs or inflicting all the pain the body can take (not that it is legal to do any of this anyway!). None of that will be of any use to you whatever. Sin will still rise up within you.

What else? Were you to weep sorrowful buckets over your sins, or Christ's suffering, or if you were to ponder limitlessly the joys of heaven, what good would it do? Surely a great deal of benefit would come to you and you would receive much grace. But in comparison with this blind stirring of love within you, there is little all those things can do for you. Love alone is the best part and it is the part Mary chose (see Luke 10:42). Without it all else is worthless. Not only does it succeed in destroying sin's roots, its very essence, but it produces virtue. If this love is truly present in you, then you will also know perfect and true goodness without any mixed motives. A man may have as many virtues as he pleases but without this love they will all be tainted, imperfect.

For virtue is no more than an ordered, deliberate love clearly directed towards God for his own sake. And God is himself the pure cause of all virtue. In fact, should anyone be motivated to seek virtue for mixed reasons, even if the chief one were God, then that renders the virtue imperfect. This can be seen from the examples of the two virtues of love and humility. Anyone possessing these has everything: he needs no more.

13 Humility, perfect and imperfect

Now, first take humility. Let's see how it is imperfect when motives are mixed, even if God is its chief reason, and how it is perfect when caused by God alone. But first if we are to look at this whole thing properly we must understand the nature of humility: then only will it be possible to assess it truly.

Humility is nothing more than an accurate self-assessment, an awareness of oneself as one really is. And surely, anyone seeing himself for what he really is, must be truly humble.

Two things cause humility. One is the state of degradation, wretchedness and weakness to which man has fallen because of sin, and of which he will always to some extent remain conscious in this life, however holy he may be. The other is the superabundant love and worth of God himself: all nature trembles, all scholars are fools, all saints and angels blind in the face of it. So much so, that if God had not portioned out their vision of him to correspond with their progress in grace, I could not describe what would happen to them.

This second cause, the love and worth of God, is the 'perfect' one because it is eternal. The former is 'imperfect' because it ends with this life. Often a soul which is still in his mortal body will find that his longing for God so increases, by God's grace, that, suddenly, he becomes oblivious of himself, not dwelling on whether he has been good or bad. Whether this occurs often or seldom, this longing impulse never lasts long. During this time he is perfectly humbled, for he knows no cause but the chief one, God himself. But when this longing is moved by other motives, even if God is the chief one, then humility remains imperfect. Still, this is good and should be experienced. God forbid that you should think otherwise.

14 Imperfect humility followed by perfection

Now although I may call it 'imperfect' humility, I would prefer that I had such an understanding and self awareness, than not. I suspect it would bring me to 'perfect' humility, its cause and power, far more quickly than if all heaven's angels and saints, plus the entire Holy Church on earth were to join together for the sole purpose of praying to God for me to achieve perfect humility!

Indeed, it is impossible for a sinner to receive and retain perfect humility without first achieving imperfect humility. So, strain every muscle in working hard to know and realise your true self. Then, I suspect, it will not be long before you have a true experience of God as he is – not as he is in himself, of course, for it is impossible for anyone but God to know that, and not as you will know him in heaven – but as far as true knowledge of him is possible for a humble soul on earth to experience, and as much as God will permit.

So don't think, because I've stated two causes of perfect humility, that I'd like you to reject the hard work of imperfect humility and to concentrate exclusively on the perfect. I'm just going through each step here because I want to show you that the worth of this spiritual exercise is greater than that of any other physical or spiritual work which can be performed by God's grace. This secret pure love of the soul, as it continues to press against this dark cloud of unknowing between you and God, sweetly and completely contains within itself that perfect humility. And I want also to show you what this humility consists of: to place it before you as an aim for your heart to love, both for your own sake and mine. For I want this knowledge to make you even more humble.

Often a lack of knowledge is the cause of so much pride! Quite likely, if you did not know what perfect humility was, you would think with your smattering of knowledge and experience of what I call 'imperfect' humility, that you had arrived! You would deceive yourself into imagining that you were truly humble, when, in fact, you were totally engulfed by your own foul pride! So work at it, try hard to come to a perfect humility. Such is its nature that whoever is in possession of it will not sin.

15 A proof against an error concerning perfection

Believe me when I say that there is this perfect humility, and that it can be obtained in this life by the grace of God. I say this to refute the error that claims perfect humility comes as a result of remembering our wretchedness and past sins.

I grant that, for habitual sinners (and I include myself), it is both essential and effective to be humbled by such rememberances, and to remain so until the sin is removed from our minds and consciences. But to those who are 'innocents', who have never habitually or deliberately committed deadly sin but only perhaps through ignorance or weakness, there are other ways by which they may come to humility. This is true of the contemplative, when his conscience or counsellor can say of him that he has truly mended his ways, by contrition, confession and penance, according to the rules of Holy Church. This perfect way to humility is quite beyond the other, as the life of Christ is beyond that of any man; or as the life of the angel who has never known, nor will ever know, human weakness, is beyond the realm of the weakest man on earth.

If there were no perfect way to be humbled except by a knowledge of one's wretchedness, I would like to know what made Jesus Christ humble – for he knew no sin. It is to this total perfection in all things that the Lord Jesus Christ himself calls us in the Gospel, when he bids us to be perfect, by grace, as he himself is by nature (see Matt. 5:48).

16   The surest way to perfection and forgiveness

Let no one dare to presume that he who was the most wretched sinner of all, just because he has now changed his ways and has been called to contemplation, by agreement of his mind and conscience, can therefore press upon the cloud of unknowing between him and God. For our Lord said to Mary Magdalene, representative of all sinners who are called to the contemplative life: 'Your sins are forgiven you.' This was not because of her great sorrow, or her preoccupation with her sin, nor even because of her humility that came as a result of her preoccupation. Why then? Surely because she loved much.

This, then, is the point where we can see how a secret fixing of love may grasp hold of our Lord better than anything else a man may do or think. I grant you that Mary greatly repented of her sins, that she wept sorely for them and that she was truly humbled at the thought of them. So we, who are wretched sinners like her, must also show repentance, sorrow and humility in the face of our own failures.

How? As Mary did, surely. Though she may not always have had the same deep heartfelt anguish for her sins, all her life she carried their burden with her wherever she went. Nevertheless, scripture clearly confirms that her sorrow, her longing, her sighing, her languishing were all the more intensified, and almost fatal, because of her desire to love God. Yet she was full of love and still longed for more love. Of course, this should come as no surprise. For we know that it is the mark of every lover that the more he loves, the more he longs to love.

Yet Mary knew full well that she was the worst of all sinners, that it was her sin that formed a gulf between herself and her beloved God, and that this was the chief cause of her inability to love God, despite her longing. So what did she do? Did she descend from the heights of love's desire to examine closely her base, foul, sinful life, turning the filth over to brood and weep over each sin as she individually recalled it? Certainly not! God had let her know by his grace within her soul that she could never come close to him this way. Much more likely she would have fallen into sin again through it.

So, instead, she clung with love and desire to this cloud of unknowing and learned to love what, in this world, she would never clearly understand through reason, nor feel the sweetness of by the emotions. So much so that in her great love she may even have forgotten that she had once been a sinner. Yes, indeed, I'm sure that so deeply did Mary love God that she was unaware of the beauty and loveliness of his physical body when he sat speaking to her (precious and blessed though it

42

was, as anything physical and spiritual can be). This seems to me to be what the Gospel is teaching here.

17 The life of the true contemplative

In Luke's Gospel we read that when our Lord visited Mary and Martha's home, while Martha was occupied preparing the evening meal, Mary, her sister, sat at his feet. As she listened to his words, she became oblivious not only of the fact that her sister was busy (albeit engaged in good holy work, which is the first part of the active life), but also of the physical aspects of Christ's manhood: his perfect blessed physique, his beautiful voice and holy words (the higher part of the active life and lower part of the contemplative). What, in fact, she was seeing beyond all this, was the sovereign wisdom of his Godhead covered over by his human words.

This is what Mary gazed upon, enraptured. Nothing she saw or heard, nothing that was going on around her, could move her. She sat rooted to the spot, reaching out with her secret, sweet, eager love towards that high cloud of unknowing that was between her and God. Let me tell you: never in this life has there been a display of a pure consuming love of God that does not come up against this high and wonderful cloud. This was the same cloud in which Mary experienced those secret moments in love. This is the sublimest state of contemplation one can know on earth, the most holy. From this state nothing could move her – so much so that her sister Martha complained about her to the Lord! She asked him to tell her sister to get up and give her a hand so that she did not have to do so much. Mary, however, remained still, said nothing, nor showed the least sign of grumbling in response to her sister's complaints. And this is not at all surprising, for she had a work to do that Martha knew nothing about. She had no spare moment to attend to Martha or even to answer her!

Look, my friend, at all that happened between our Lord and these two sisters: here is an example of all actives and contemplatives who have followed the Christian way, and it shall continue on to Judgment Day. Mary stands for all the contemplatives: they take their pattern from her. And Martha represents the actives.

18   A complaint born of ignorance

Just as Martha complained of Mary her sister, right up to this day all actives complain of contemplatives. For if anyone in the whole world, irrespective of class or creed, feels deeply stirred within, by grace and good counsel, to forsake all outward forms of work and to totally engage in a contemplative way of living, then, as soon as he or she does so, their own brothers and sisters, close friends, and others who know nothing whatever of this calling, all rise up with a great hue and cry and complain strongly, telling him not to waste his time. They conjure up all kinds of strange tales, some true, some false, of how this person, and that person, who had devoted their lives to contemplation, had fallen by the wayside. There's not a good word about those who've succeeded.

Certainly, many people who have seemed to forsake the world do fall. That's quite true. They should have become servants of God as contemplatives but, because they were unable to maintain their spiritual discipline, they have become contemplatives of the devil and his servants. They have become heretics, hypocrites, fanatics and so on, undermining the Church. I will not enlarge on this. It will take us away from the subject. Another time perhaps, God willing, we may look at their condition and the reasons why they fell away. But let's say no more for now: press on!

19 Good reason to excuse an accusation

Some people will say that I pay Martha scant respect: that I've compared the complaints of that special saint with those of outright worldly men. I truly mean no dishonour to her or the others. God forbid that I should, here or elsewhere, in any way condemn God's servants, especially this special saint. I think, in fact, that we can excuse her complaint when we understand the circumstances in which she said it. She spoke in ignorance. And no wonder, for she did not realise what Mary was doing; she probably had never before come across this work of perfection. And what she said was courteous and to the point. Indeed, we must completely exonerate Martha!

Similarly, I think, the other, worldly, men and women, should also be excused, even if they put their complaints rudely. They too are ignorant. They have no idea what these young disciples of God mean when they let go of this world and withdraw to become God's special servants, in holiness, and rightness of spirit. If they but knew, I dare say they would never behave or speak as they do. Further, when I consider my own innumerable faults in word and deed, which I have often committed through ignorance, I remember that if I am to be excused by God for these sins of ignorance, then I too must always in love and forgiveness excuse similar words and acts of others. Surely I must do to others as I would they should do to me.

20 God answers those who persist with him

Therefore, I think, those who decide to become contemplatives should not only excuse active men their complaints, but they should be so spiritually busy that they have no time to be concerned with what others say and do to them. Mary is the example again: if we truly do the same, our

Lord will do for us what he did then for Mary (see Luke 10:38–41).

This is what he did: our loving Lord Jesus Christ, from whom no secret is hidden, answered on Mary's behalf. When Martha asked him to become judge by telling Mary to get up and to help her serve him, he saw through into everything, he saw that Mary's spirit was devoutly intent upon loving his Godhead. So, with great courtesy, he replied on Mary's behalf: her love was so intense that she could not break away from him. How did Jesus reply? Certainly not as the judge, as Martha had expected, but as an advocate, defending the one who so loved him.

'Martha, Martha!' – he called her by name twice, so eager was he that she should listen to his words. 'You are very busy,' he said, 'and troubled by many things.'

He said this to Martha wanting her to know that her work was good and of benefit to her soul. Actives have to be busy and worried about a number of things to provide for their own needs and for their good deeds of love and mercy to fellow Christians. But he also wanted to tell her that it was not the best or highest thing one could do. He said: 'But one thing is necessary.'

And what is that one thing? Surely, it is to cast aside all other activity and to worship and love God for himself. Jesus wanted to stop Martha thinking that she could love and praise God above all else and still be busily occupied with the everyday affairs of life. So he settled the question about whether spiritual and physical pursuits could be held together (imperfectly maybe, but not perfectly), by adding: 'Mary has chosen the best part, which shall never be taken from her.' For the perfect outreaching of love to God begun here in this life is the same as that which shall last into life eternal, in the bliss of heaven, for it is all one. ('Faith and hope give way to vision; but the life of love begun here, is continued uninterrupted in heaven.' 1 Cor. 13)

What did Jesus mean when he said to Martha: 'Mary has chosen the best part'? Whenever 'the best' is stated, it implies that there is a good and a better; so the best is the third thing. So what are the three things of which Mary chose 'the best'? They can't be three lives, for Holy Church knows only two: the active and the contemplative. Insight into both these ways of living can already be gleaned from the Gospel story of Mary and Martha: Martha the active and Mary the contemplative. Without one of these two lives, no one can be saved, and if there are no more than two, no one can choose 'the best'.

But though there are only two lives between them, there are three parts, each one better than the other. These have been mentioned in correct order earlier in the book.

The first part of the active life consists of good honest works of mercy and charity. Then there is good spiritual meditation on our own sinfulness, the sufferings of Christ and the joy of heaven: they are the second part of the active life and the first part of the contemplative life which overlap to form the second part. It is better than the first part of the active life. Here we see their common ground. An active may rise to the heights of contemplation – and on rare occasions, by grace, reach its pinnacle. The contemplative can at times descend to this level of active life, but no lower – except in times of great need, which are very rare. The third part is caught up in secret love to God in this dark cloud of unknowing.

The first part is good, the second part is better, the third part is best of all. This is the part which Mary chose and of which the Lord spoke to Martha. He said of this third part, 'It shall never be taken from her.' The first and second parts are, therefore, to end with this life, despite their worth and holiness. For in heaven there will be no need to show works of mercy and charity, or to weep for our sinfulness or for

Christ's sufferings; no man shall hunger or thirst any more, nor die of cold or be sick, homeless, in prison, or die and be buried. The third part that Mary chose must be chosen by all called to this way of life. Or, to put it more accurately: whoever is chosen for that part of life by God, should follow its way with energy and enthusiasm. For it shall never be taken from him.

So, let the voice of the Lord be heard amongst these actives as if it were being said now for us, as it was then for Mary to Martha, 'Martha! Martha! Actives! Actives! Get on with your busy lives if you feel it is right and live in both parts with courage. But leave my contemplatives to me. Don't interfere with their way, for you do not know what is happening to them. Leave them in their repose and pleasure, in the third part and the best part of life that Mary chose.'

22 From conversion to contemplation

Sweet it was, that love between Mary and our Lord Jesus: so much love she had for him, yet much more had he for her. Whoever really wants to know what passed between them – as the true Gospel testifies, not just as any superficial story teller might suggest – will discover the deep love that Mary poured upon Jesus because nothing else besides him could satisfy her longing soul, nor could anything else distract her heart from him.

This is the same Mary[1] who, when she looked for him weeping at the sepulchre, would not be comforted by the angels. Even when so gently and lovingly they said: 'Weep

---

[1]It is now believed that Mary (the sister of Martha) and Mary Magdalene were not the same person. It was Mary of Magdala who went to the tomb with the other Mary (also called Mary, mother of James), of whom we know little. Ed. note.

not, Mary, for our Lord, whom you seek, is risen, and you shall have him and see him alive in all his beauty, among his disciples in Galilee, just as he said' (Matt. 28:1–7; John 20:11–13). She would still not stop crying because she thought that anyone truly seeking the King of angels would not stop crying for mere angels!

What more? Surely anyone who truly wants to understand the Gospel story will find many wonderful things of perfect love written about her as an example to us. It's almost as if they'd been recorded just for this book, so exactly do they tally with my purpose in writing! Indeed, they were, whatever one may say. If one could see in the Gospel story that wonderful and special love our Lord had for Mary, who represents all sincere converts called to contemplation, one will see how impossible it was for our Lord to let anyone speak a word against her, not even her own sister. In fact he took it upon himself to defend her. Further, he rebuked Simon the leper in his own house because he had criticised her in his mind (see Luke 7:36 ff).[2] This is great love: indeed, surpassing love.

23 God provides for those who love him

Without a doubt our Lord will speak up for us even today if we truly pattern our love and life style upon Mary's way, and do our best, helped by God's grace. I cannot say that we won't have our critics. As long as we are in this suffering world, people will think or say something against us. But I do say that if we ignore it all and remain faithful to our spiritual calling, as did Mary, then our Lord will speak to the hearts of those who are sincere in their criticism. He will answer them

---

[2]Mary of Bethany (the sister of Martha) did anoint Jesus's feet but this is not the occasion when Simon criticises the woman in Luke 7:36 ff. Ed. note.

in such a way that they will soon be ashamed of their thoughts and words.

Just as he answers for us in spirit, so will he also stir others in spirit to provide for our needs in food, clothing and so on when they see our inability to leave our work to attend to these matters. I want to say this in order to refute those who say that it is wrong to serve God in contemplation unless one has first made adequate provision for oneself. They quote the saying, 'God sends the cow, but not by the horn,' meaning, 'God helps those who help themselves.' This, as they well know, maligns God. You can be absolutely confident, whoever you are, that if you have renounced the world for God, then, without you doing anything at all, he will send you one of two things: either more than you need, or the physical strength and spiritual patience to endure deprivation. And what does it matter which of the two you have? It is all the same to the true contemplative. Anybody who doubts this has either been wrenched from his faith by the devil within him or he does not really belong to God as he should. This principle is true of everyone, no matter who he is or what righteous reasons he puts forward.

So you – who, like Mary, set yourself the task of contemplation – choose rather to be humbled by the supreme, holy and perfect God than by your own sinful unworthiness. Those who are perfectly humble lack nothing, spiritually or physically. They possess all in God. And as this book keeps saying, such a person needs nothing else in life.

24 The nature of love revealed in contemplation

So, as I have said, humility is mysteriously and perfectly understood in this little blind love of God, beating away at the dark cloud of unknowing, all else forgotten. And this applies to all other virtues, especially love.

Love means loving God for himself alone, first, above all else, and loving others as oneself. In contemplation God is loved in this way: nothing else is sought. There is a naked intent, a single-mindedness of spirit, directed towards God alone.

A 'naked intent' I call it, because in this work a perfect apprentice asks for neither a release from pain, nor ample reward, nor anything else, but God himself. So much so that he doesn't care at all whether he is in pain or bliss, but simply that the will of God, whom he loves, be fulfilled. In this work a contemplative may not entertain any thought of even the holiest creature God ever made to rival him.

As he does this, the second, and lower, branch of charity, which is love to one's fellow Christian, is properly fulfilled, as can be proved. For in perfect contemplation everyone is regarded equally. No man, whether relative, friend, stranger or foe, is specially loved. All are considered friends, no one an enemy – so much so that the contemplative even reckons to describe as real and special friends those who may hurt and injure him. He is stirred in love to wish for them as much good as he would wish his dearest friend.

25 A time of perfection in relationships

I cannot say that, in this work of contemplation, one should have a special regard for someone, be he friend or foe, relative or stranger, because all but God is to be completely forgotten. What I do say, however, is that the contemplative will be so full of virtue and love that – even later, when he comes down from his mountain tops to talk or pray with his fellow Christians – his attitude and will towards others, relatives or strangers, friend or foe, will be still perfectly directed by

God. Not that he ever ought to come away from such a close encounter with God. That would not be right at all. But on occasion he has, out of love for others, to make that descent. Indeed, when he does, then it is possible that he will attend more to his enemy than his friend!

Anyway, in this work of loving God he has no leisure time to consider who are his friends and who his enemies. And, of course, he will often feel greater affection for a few; that is true for many reasons. Christ felt closer love for John, Mary and Peter than for others. But what I'm saying is that, when caught up in contemplation, then all people become of equal importance because one feels nothing but God. All are then simply and openly loved for God's sake as well as their own.

All men are lost in Adam and show by their works their desire for salvation and are saved only by the fact of Christ's suffering. Yet, as experience suggests this, the soul totally disposed towards contemplation, and thus united with God in Spirit, performs whatever is necessary to make all men as perfect as itself. When a limb of the body feels pain or well-being so all the other limbs suffer distress or feel well. That's how it is with the spiritual 'limbs' of the body of Holy Church. Christ is its head, we are the limbs if we join the body in love. Anyone who wants to be a perfect disciple of our Lord's must train to perfection in this spiritual life for the purpose of bringing salvation to all his brothers and sisters in this world, as did our Lord by his death on the cross. He did this not just for his family and friends but for all mankind, irrespective of who they are. And everyone who turns away from sin and asks God's forgiveness shall be saved by the fact of Christ's suffering and death.

What is understood of humility and love is true of all virtues. They are all sweetly included in that little act of love which we have already touched on.

So work hard and fast at this work of contemplation, beating upon this cloud of unknowing – and rest later! It's going to be very hard work, make no mistake, unless the contemplative has special grace given him, or he has been practising this for some time.

But what is this hard work? It is certainly not that stirring of love which comes from Almighty God mounting up within him. It is not self-inspired but what God causes in each willing soul doing everything possible to equip himself for this work.

The hard work is undoubtedly the grind of suppressing all those other thoughts that surge up; the effort of holding them down under the cloud of forgetting. This is where man's hard work lies, and it can be endured only by God's grace. The stirring of love is entirely the work of God. So carry on your end. I can promise you that, on his side, God will not fail.

Work with speed, then; let me see how you bear up. Can you not see that God awaits you? Shame on you! Work, then, speedily for a while, and soon the pressure will ease: the task will not feel so enormous and laborious. Though at the outset, when your devotion is small, the work is difficult and restricting, later, as your love for God deepens, you will find rest and release, and it will be light and sometimes effortless. Then God will sometimes do it all for you. But not always or for very long; God works when and how he pleases and you will be happy for him to do so.

At such times he may send out flashes of spiritual light piercing this cloud of unknowing which lies between you and him, illuminating the soul. You will not be able to speak of the secrets God reveals to you then. It is impossible and it is forbidden. God will set you on fire with such desire for his love, that I cannot write about it here. Those things are all for God alone to show you: I dare not take it upon myself to tell you of them, blabbering on with this unworthy earthly tongue. Yet gladly I would tell you of the part men play in this work, helped by God's grace, for that subject is less fraught with danger.

27 Who should engage in this work of grace?

First and foremost, let me tell you who should practise contemplation, and when and how and under what conditions. As to who, I reply: 'Everyone who has truly, purposefully forsaken the world, giving themselves not just to active living, but to the contemplative life. A man or woman may embark upon this life even though he or she has previously been a habitual sinner.'

28 A cleansing first before contemplation

If you were to ask me when a person should contemplate, I would answer: 'Only when the conscience has been cleansed of all sin, according to the general rules of Holy Church.'

In contemplation a soul dries up the residue of sin, which inevitably lingers on despite confession and however hard he tries. But anyone working at being a contemplative must first cleanse his conscience and then draw boldly, albeit humbly, to his work, very conscious of the length of time he has been kept away from it. For this is the work in which a soul should labour all his life whether or not he had never committed a deadly sin. All the while a soul lives in its mortal body he shall experience the difficulties of this cloud of unknowing between him and his God. Moreover, he will see and feel the distraction of the world in his mind, coming between him and his God as a result of original sin.

54

Man, the sovereign and lord of all creation, has disobeyed God, choosing to serve creation rather than its Creator. Because of this, it is in God's wisdom and justice that the man who chooses to obey God's call (i.e. to contemplate) experiences that very same creation proudly rising above him to come between him and his God.

29 To continue, to suffer, to judge no one

So if a man really desires his lost innocence, and seeks to win through to that wholeness where grief is no more, he must – whoever he is, sinner or not – obediently strive to do this work, suffering its pain.

All men find this work laborious, sinners and so-called innocents alike. But, understandably, for the former it is much harder work. Yet it often happens that the hardened habitual sinners come sooner to perfect contemplation than those who have hardly sinned at all. It is, indeed, by a merciful miracle of our Lord, who gives them this special grace to the world's amazement. I really do believe that the Day of Judgment, when God and his gifts will be clearly and openly seen, will be glorious. Those who are now despised and dismissed, because they are common or even vile sinners, shall on that day sit with the saints in God's sight. And those who now appear so holy and are worshipped, by some men, as angelic beings who never committed a mortal sin, will sit in sorrow in the devil's caves.

So you see that, in this life, no man should be judged by others on the basis of the good or evil he has done. By all means, the deed can be judged to be good or bad, but not the man.

30 Who can judge others' faults?

Who then can judge the deeds of others? Surely only those who have the authority and care for their souls. This responsibility may either be given by the law and ordinances of Holy Church, or else privately and spiritually by the special stirring by the Holy Spirit in perfect love. Each man should beware. He must not presume to take it upon himself to blame and condemn another man's faults unless he is absolutely sure that he is moved within by the Holy Spirit. Otherwise he might very well be completely mistaken. So be extremely careful. Judge yourself, if you will, before God and your father in God. But leave others alone.

31 A beginner's behaviour

When you feel you have done all that the Church has told you in order to put yourself in the right with God, get to work quick sharp! If memories of your past keep coming between you and your God, or if any new thought or sin arises, tread heavily over them, crushing them down by your fervent love of God. Cover them with a thick cloud of forgetting by behaving as if they didn't exist. Suppress them, however often they arise. When it gets really difficult, use every trick in the book, every spiritual device, to overcome them. Such art is better learned from God by experience than from any man in this life.

32 Two spiritual ploys

Let me tell you, however, what I know of these arts. Try them out and see if you can improve on them!

First, act and behave as though you haven't an inkling that they are driving so hard to come between you and your God. Try, as it were, to look over their shoulders. Stare past them seeking something else (which is God, enclosed in a cloud of unknowing). If you do this, I believe you will soon find your work easier, for seen correctly it is none other than a longing desire to feel and see God, as one may, even here on earth. Such desire is love and always deserves to have its way made easier.

There is a second device you can try out. When you feel powerless to overcome these thoughts and images, cower down before them like a cringing coward defeated in battle, and reckon it stupid to fight them any longer. In this way in the very hand of the enemy, you yield yourself to God. Note this carefully, I pray, for I think that if you try it out you will dissolve all opposition. This ploy, too, when looked at rightly will be seen as nothing less than a true realisation of the self as a wretched, filthy thing that is worse than nothing. Such self-knowledge and awareness is humility. This causes God to come down in his great might to avenge your enemies, to lift you up again lovingly and dry your spiritual eyes, just as a father would his child who is about to die in the jaws of a wild boar or mad biting bears.

33 A sinner is cleansed, but sin remains

I shall not, for the time being, tell you of any more skills, for if you are given grace to test these out, I'm sure that you will soon be teaching me more than I you! Although I've been able to teach you, I am far from knowing it all myself. So I ask you to help me as well as yourself.

Keep on working hard and as fast as you can, I pray. If at first you don't win through with these ploys, suffer the pain humbly. Truly, it is your purgatory. When the pain has passed and these skills, given to you by God in grace, become a habit, then I have no doubt that you will be cleansed not only from sin but also from the suffering it brings.

I am referring, here, to your past deliberate sins, not to original sin: the suffering of that will remain with you until death, no matter how hard you work in this life. Still, that pain is minor compared with the suffering caused by your deliberate sins. Each day will bring its own new uprising of sin which you will have to force down constantly. Work hard. Smite at it with the double-edged sword of discernment and caution. As you do all this you will learn that there is no real security or true rest in this life.

However, you must not draw back or feel too much fear of failure. For if by grace you destroy the pain of your past sins (as I've described or, preferably, in your own way, if it is better), you can be sure that the pain of original sin or the new risings of sin it will still produce, will be of little trouble to you.

34 God's grace is free, not earned

If you asked me how you should begin contemplation, I would pray for Almighty God to teach you himself by his immense grace and kindness. Indeed, it is important that you know that I cannot teach you. This is not surprising: this is the work of God. He will bring it about in whichever soul he pleases, irrespective of its merits. Without God's grace neither saint nor angel could ever begin to think of desiring the life of contemplation. And I believe that our Lord will do this work as readily as often, and perhaps even more often, in habitual sinners than in those who, by comparison, seem to have hardly sinned at all. He will do this to show us that he is the almighty, all-merciful God who is free to do as he pleases.

Yet God cannot begin this work in a soul that is unable to receive it, no more than a soul could have this grace unless

God gives it. It is not given as a reward for one's innocence nor withheld for one's sin. Note that I do not say 'withdrawn' but rather 'withheld'. Beware of error here; the more man touches upon the truth, the more he must be on guard against error. I think my meaning is clear but if you cannot understand it, lay it aside until God teaches you. Don't worry about it.

Beware of pride: it blasphemes God and his gifts, and encourages sinners. If you were truly humble, you would feel as I do about the contemplative life: God gives it freely, regardless of merit.

The nature of contemplation is such that when it comes, the soul can both practise it and know it is doing so. It is impossible to have it otherwise. The capacity for contemplation and the act itself are one and the same thing. Only the person who feels able to contemplate, can, in fact, do so; nobody else. Without this prior working of God, the soul is dead, and unable to covet or desire it. Since you will and desire it, you have it, but it is not from yourself that this comes: where it comes from and where it leads to is something unknown. Don't be afraid that you may never know more than this, but keep going and you will continue to advance.

In short, let this unknown deal with you and lead you as it will. Let it do the work, you follow its lead. Watch, if you like, but leave it alone. Do not interfere with it, for fear of spoiling it, even though you may want to help. Be the tree, let it be the carpenter. Be the house, let it be the resident owner. Be blind, as it were, yielding all desire to know, for knowledge will be a hindrance rather than a help. It is more than enough that you should feel this sweet stirring of inner love by this unknown, that in it you should have no real thought for anything less than God, and that you should direct that naked intent upon God.

And if this is all true of you, then you can be confident that it is God himself who directly stirs your will and desire. Have no fear, the devil cannot come near you. Sometimes he may arouse your will but even then only from a distance, no matter how subtly devilish he may be! Without due authority not even a good angel may direct your will. Indeed, nothing but God can.

You can understand to some extent by what I've written, but even more clearly by experience, that men come direct to contemplation with the help of no other. All aid is dependent upon it, but it does not depend upon help in any way.

35 The practice of reading, thinking and praying

Having said all that, there are helps which the apprentice contemplative can employ: lesson, meditation and orison. Put more simply: reading, thinking and praying. These you will find written about in another book[1] by someone else, much better than I could ever tell you, so I shall not go into them here. But I will just mention one thing: they are all so interdependent that – for beginners and proficients, but not for the perfect (as much as is possible in this life) – thinking will come only after first reading or hearing. Reading and hearing are the same for everyone: clergy read books, and the lay man 'reads' the clergy when he hears from them the word of God. Prayer also can only follow on after thinking.

Put it to the test: God's word, written or spoken, can be likened to a mirror. Spiritually, the 'eye' of your soul is your reason. Your conscience is your spiritual 'face'. Just as you cannot see a dirty spot on your physical face without the aid of a mirror, or someone telling you, so it is with your 'spiritual'

---

[1]The book referred to is perhaps the *Scala Claustralium*, which was translated into English in the fourteenth century as *A ladder of four rungs, by the which ladder men will climb to heaven.* The four rungs – lesson, meditation, orison and contemplation – are interdependent.

face. Man is so blinded by his continual sin that, without reading or hearing God's word, it is impossible for him to see that his conscience has dirty marks on it.

It follows, then, that only if a man sees sin's dirty mark on his soul can he run off to the well of Holy Church to wash himself with the water of confession. If sin is deeply rooted, producing evil impulses, then the 'well' is all-merciful God, and the 'water' prayer – with all that that involves.

So you can see how, for all beginners and proficients, reading or hearing is the first step, thinking the next and then follows prayer.

36   Meditations of the contemplative

But all this is not true for the contemplatives. For them, meditation is the sudden recognition and groping awareness of their own wretchedness, or of the goodness of God, without the aid of hearing or reading blessed thoughts usual in meditation.

This sudden perception and awareness is better learned from God than man. I do not mind if, at this stage, you have no other meditations about your own wretchedness or God's goodness than those which come through a single word like 'sin' or 'God', for I assume you are moved by God's grace and direction in all this. Do not analyse or expound these words by clever inventiveness, imagining that considering these words will increase your devotion. I believe this type of thinking should never occur in contemplation. Rather, take the words whole.

By 'sin' mean the whole 'lump' of it, nothing other than your whole self. I think that in this instinctive awareness of sin thus solidified into a lump, which is none other than yourself, you will discover the maddest person on earth, desperate for restraint! Yet any onlooker will think from your appearance that you are perfectly sober, self-controlled in body, giving no trace of anything other than perfect calm in your behaviour, manner or expression, whether you are sitting, walking, lying down, leaning, standing or kneeling.

37 Special prayers of the contemplative

Just as the meditations of the contemplative rise suddenly, unaided, so, too, do their prayers. I refer to their private prayers, of course, not to those set down by Holy Church. True contemplatives could not value more highly the prayers of Holy Church and they use them in the form and according to the regulations ordained by the holy fathers before us. But their special private prayers rise spontaneously to God, without special aid or premeditation as they pray the set prayers.

And when these spontaneous prayers are in words, as they seldom are, those words are few; indeed, the fewer the better. In fact, one word of a single syllable rather than two, is more in accordance with the spirit. For a contemplative should always live at the highest, topmost peak spiritually. An earthly example illustrates the truth of this principle: a person suddenly afraid of fire or death is driven to cry out or pray for help. Surely he is not going to use a whole lot of words, or even only a word of two syllables! It would waste too much time. So he bursts out in his terror and urgent need with a cry of one little word of one single syllable – like 'Fire!' or 'Help!'.

Just as a short cry of 'Fire' stirs and pierces the ears of those who hear it, so a little word of one syllable expresses the secret depths of the spirit's longing, even when it is not stated in words or thought. It is secretly expressed in the depth of the spirit – which is also its height, length and breadth. This pierces the ears of Almighty God more quickly than any long psalm reiterated meaninglessly. So, the saying goes, 'Short prayer pierces heaven.'

38 Short prayer pierces heaven

Why does this short prayer of one syllable penetrate heaven? Surely because it is prayed with a full spirit – that is, in the height, depth, length and breadth of the spirit of the one that prays. In the height, for it is with all the might of his spirit; in the depth, for in it is contained all that the spirit knows; in the length, for should it always feel as it does now, ever would it cry out as it now cries; in the breadth, for it extends to all others what it wills for itself.

At this time the soul understands what St Paul and the other saints speak of (not fully, but as clearly as is possible at this stage of contemplation): what is the length, the breadth, the height and the depth of everlasting, all-lovely, almighty, all-knowing God. The everlastingness of God is his length; his love is his breadth; his might is his height; his wisdom is his depth. No wonder that a soul brought so close by the transforming grace of God into the likeness of its own Maker should so soon be heard by God! Yes, even though it is a soul full of sin and an enemy of God as it were, if by grace he were to cry that little syllable in the height, depth, length and breadth of his spirit, then he would always be heard and helped by God because of his anguished cry.

We see this from an example. If you heard your deadly enemy cry out in terror from the depth of his being 'Fire!' or 'Help!', then you would respond out of sheer pity. It would not matter that he was your enemy. It wouldn't even matter if it were at the dead of night in mid-winter, the despair of his cry would stir you to put out his fire, or to quieten and ease his distress. Oh, Lord! Since grace may make a man so merciful that he shows such pity and mercy to his enemy, what pity and mercy shall God have for the spiritual cry of a soul delivered in its height, depth, length and breadth? God has, by nature, all that man possesses by grace and much more. God has incomparably more mercy than man since mercy is essential to God's nature, whereas by grace it comes to man later on.

39 The nature and practice of prayer

We must pray in the height, depth, length and breadth of the spirit without many words but with one word of one syllable. That word must be best suited to the nature of prayer itself, and before we can select such a word we must first understand what prayer is.

Prayer is nothing other than a devout intent directed to God in order that one may gain goodness and banish evil. Since all evil is summed up in sin, either by cause or in being, we should pray for the removing of evil. But in this prayer do not waste time thinking about the subject. Do not say much. Use only this little word 'sin'. If we pray for goodness, then let us cry, with word or thought or desire, nothing but that one word 'God'. For in God is all good; he is its beginning and its existence.

Do not be surprised, then, that I give these two words priority. If I knew any shorter words that so completely summed up good and evil as these do, or if God had taught me other words, then I would have used these instead. And that is my advice to you. Don't make a study of words, for you will never achieve your purpose or be able to contemplate that way. Contemplation is never attained by study, but by grace. And, despite what I've said, use your own words which God has led you to use for prayer. And if God directs you to use those I've given you, I advise you not to let go of them (that is, if you pray in words, not otherwise, of course).

They are very short words, and though I recommend the short prayer, its frequency is not to be curtailed. For, as I've already said, prayer is made in the length of the spirit. So prayer should never cease until it finally and completely possesses that for which the soul longs. We can see this from our example of the terrified man or woman: they do not stop crying 'Help!' or 'Fire!' until they have got all the help they need in their trouble.

40 In contemplation a soul is unaware of special vice or virtue

In the same way you should fill your spirit with the spiritual meaning of the word 'sin', without analysing whether it is venial or mortal: pride, anger, envy, covetousness, sloth, gluttony or lust. What does it matter to contemplatives what sin it is or how great? To them, at the time of contemplation, all sins alike are major, beginning from the smallest sin which separates them from God and prevents inner peace.

Feel sin as a lump of nothing else but yourself! Recognise the whole of you as sin, then always cry in your spirit this one thing: 'Sin! Sin! Sin! Help! Help! Help!' Such spiritual cries are better learned from God by experience than from any man by word. It is best when they are purely spiritual, and unpremeditated, and unuttered except for rare moments when the spirit, filled with sorrow and the burden of sin, overflows and bursts into words.

It is in the same way that you must use this little word 'God'. Fill your spirit with its inner meaning, paying little attention to any of God's works – not analysing whether they be good, better or best, physical or spiritual. Do not think about any virtue which has been wrought in a man's soul by grace, wondering whether it is humility or charity, patience, abstinence, hope, faith, self-control, chastity or voluntary poverty. What does all this matter to contemplatives? In God is all virtue; contemplatives find and feel in him everything there by origin and by continuation. They know that if they have God they possess all good, so they do not covet any special thing, but only God, who is all good. You should do the same, as far as you are able by grace, and intend to find God with your whole being and the whole of God so that nothing works in your mind or will but God alone.

And because – all the while that you live this wretched life – you must feel, in some way, this foul nauseating lump of sin as part and parcel of yourself, you must all your life turn alternatively to these two words 'sin' and 'God'. You can know this: if you had God you would not have sin, and if you did not have sin, then you would have God!

41 Restraint in everything else but contemplation

If you should ask me what restraint you should exercise in this work, I would answer, 'None whatever!' In all other matters you are bound to use restraint; for example, in the question of food and drink, sleeping, keeping warm or cool, in long prayers or time spent reading, or in conversation with fellow Christians. In all this you get the right balance. But in contemplation, be abandoned! I want you never to cease from this work as long as you live.

I am not saying that you can continue in it always with the same freshness; that cannot be. Illness or some other disorder of body or soul, or physical needs will greatly hinder you in contemplation, and pull you down. But you should always attend to your work in intention if not in actuality: there is no 'time off'! So, for the love of God, take care of yourself and try not to fall ill. Don't let illness be the cause of weakness on your part. I tell you honestly, contemplation demands

66

great tranquillity, wholeness, and purity in both body and soul.

So, for the love of God, discipline your body and soul alike, keeping fit and healthy. If you should get ill, through circumstances beyond your control, bear it patiently and wait patiently upon God's mercy. That is all you need do. It is true to say that patience in sickness and other forms of trouble pleases God much more than any splendid devotion that you might show in health.

42 Lack of restraint in contemplation brings restraint in all else

Perhaps you will ask me how you are to display self-control in drinking, sleeping and everything else. I will reply briefly: 'Take life as it comes.' Contemplate ceaselessly with abandonment and you will have all the discipline you need for other things. I cannot believe that a soul who works inordinately in contemplation, day and night, will err in mundane affairs. If he does, I think he's the type who would always get things wrong!

So, if I gave my whole-hearted attention to this spiritual work within me, I would then view eating and drinking, sleeping and speaking and everything else without too much concern. It is preferable to be restrained in these matters through this lack of concern than by paying great attention to them, weighing up every single possibility. Indeed, I myself would never bring it about, for all my talking and doing. Let men argue about this as they will: experience will prove it. So lift up your heart with a blind stirring of love, fully aware of sin and God in turn. You want to have God, you want to dispossess sin: God is absent but sin abounds. May the good God help you now, for you are now truly in need!

43 Knowledge and awareness recede for perfect contemplation

See to it that God alone is at work in your mind and will, and nothing else. Try to suppress all knowing and feeling that is not to do with God himself. Tread down under the cloud of forgetting everything that is less than God. Understand that in contemplation you should forget not only other people and their work for God, but also yourself and what you have done for God. It is the way of the perfect lover: to love the object of his love more than he loves himself, and also, in a way, to hate himself for the sake of that which he loves.

So it must be with you: you must hate everything in your mind and will that is not God. Otherwise, surely, that thing will come between you and your God. And do not be surprised to find that you come to loathe and hate thinking of yourself when you feel sin to be a foul nauseating lump of nothing other than yourself! Sin comes between you and your God, yet you must identify with it to the point of it being inseparable from you.

So destroy all knowledge and experience of any form of creation – of yourself above all. It is upon your self-knowledge and experience that all other knowledge and experience depends. Everything else will fall into place. If you will take the time to test it, you will find that when literally everything else fades, there still remains between you and God the stark awareness of your own being. And this too must be destroyed if you are to experience the perfection of contemplation.

44 The soul plays its part to achieve perfection

You ask next how to destroy this stark awareness of your own being. Perhaps you think that if it were destroyed all other hindrances would be destroyed too. Quite right. But I must say that, without the special grace that is fully and freely given by God, together with your own total readiness to receive it, this stark self-awareness cannot possibly be destroyed.

This readiness is nothing else than a strong, deep sorrow of the spirit. But in it you will need to exercise restraint. Beware of placing undue strain on your body or soul at such times: rather, sit completely still, as though you were asleep, exhausted and sunk in sorrow. This is true sorrow, perfect sorrow, and all will be well with you if you can achieve sorrow to such a degree. Everyone is sorrowful over something, but none more than he who truly knows himself. All other sorrow by comparison is but an imitation of the real thing. For he who knows real sorrow experiences not only what he is, but that he is. The person who has not experienced such real sorrow, should really be sorry, for he has never known perfect sorrow! This perfect sorrow, when you experience it, cleanses the soul not only of sin, but of the suffering that sin deserves. And it makes a soul able to receive that joy which lifts a man out of all awareness of his own being.

This sorrow, if it is genuine, is full of holy longing, without which a man might never be able to endure his sorrow in this life. For the soul's good strivings bring strength and comfort. Otherwise a man could not cope with what he experiences from such a deep awareness of his being. As often as he knows this true knowledge of God in purity of spirit (as far as is possible here on earth), just so often he goes nearly mad with sorrow. He feels that he may not experience God, for his awareness is occupied and filled with the foul nauseating lump of himself, which must be hated, despised and forsaken if he is to be God's perfect disciple as the Lord himself taught on the Mount of Perfection. The man weeps and wails, strives, curses and denounces himself. In brief, he thinks his burden so heavy that he doesn't care what happens to him as long as God is pleased. Yet in all this sorrow he does not want to cease to be: that would be the devil's madness and contempt for God. Though he desires desperately to be free of this awareness of his being, yet he greatly wants to continue to exist and gives God whole-hearted thanks for his precious gift.

This sorrow and this longing is felt in one way or another by every soul. God shows his favour by teaching his spiritual disciples according to his good will and they must have an accompanying readiness in body and soul, in development and disposition, before they can be perfectly at one with God in perfect love, God willing and as far as is possible in this life.

45 Certain errors to watch out for

I can tell you one thing: in this work a young disciple, inexperienced and untested spiritually, may very well be deceived. So let him beware! He must have the grace to stop and take advice humbly, otherwise he will be destroyed physically and fall into a spiritual fantasy, becoming proud, materialistic and inquisitive.

The deception may come about like this: a young man or woman, just starting in the school of devotion, hears someone read or speak about this sorrow and longing, of ceaselessly lifting up the heart to God, desiring to feel his love. Immediately they understand these words, not spiritually, as intended, but in a material physical sense. And because they lack grace and are proud and inquisitive, they strain their natural hearts most outrageously! Their whole nervous system is put under strain in this animal fashion until in less than no time they become physically and spiritually exhausted. This then causes them to turn from an inner life to seek empty, false physical comfort in so-called refreshment, in relaxation, of body and spirit! Alternatively, if they escape that trap, they get an unnatural glow and heat within, caused by the abuse of their bodies or their sham spirituality. Or again they feel a false heat brought about by the fiend, their spiritual enemy, because of their pride, materialism and human inquisitiveness. They thoroughly deserve all this; their spiritual blindness and physical discomfort is caused by their spiritual pretence and animal behaviour.

Despite all this they imagine their disturbance to be the fire of love, kindled and fanned by the grace and goodness of the Holy Spirit. In all truth, a great deal of wrong springs from such deceit: much hypocrisy, much heresy, and much error. As quickly as false knowledge follows in the fiend's school, so in God's school true experience is followed by true knowledge. For I tell you truly, the devil has his contemplatives, as God has his.

This deception in feeling and knowing takes as many weird and wonderful forms as there are diverse temperaments and conditions (as does true experience and knowledge in those who are saved). But I will include only the deceptions that will attack you if ever you mean to become a contemplative. How can it help you to know how clergy, or other men and women different from you, are led astray? Absolutely no way at all. So let me just tell you about the deceptions I believe will happen to you if you undertake this work. Then you may be on guard if they should somehow attack you.

46 Escaping the errors and working with spiritual eagerness

For the love of God take care when you embark on this work. Do not overstrain your emotions or your ability. Work with a glad zest rather than by sheer physical effort. For the more sweet and eager your work, the more humble and spiritual it becomes; the more crude, the more material and animal. So be on your guard. The animal in us that dares to touch the

71

high mountain of contemplation needs to be beaten away with stones.[1] Stones are hard, dry objects that hurt severely when they hit. These crude physical strainings spring from the hard materialistic outlook, dry from the lack of the dew of grace. They badly hurt the foolish soul, which festers in feigned fiendish fantasies!

So watch out for this animal crudeness. Learn to love with eager joy, with a softness and quietness of body and soul. Wait upon God in humility, and with quiet restraint. Do not snatch greedily like a voracious greyhound, however much you may hunger for it. If I may put it more light-heartedly: I advise you to control that great spiritual outburst so that it appears you would not have God know just how glad you are to see him, to have him, to feel him!

Perhaps this all sounds very childish. But I do believe that anyone with the grace to do as I suggest would have a lovely playful spiritual game with God, just as an earthly father does with his child, hugging and kissing him, and he would be glad to have it so.

47 Purity of spirit: the desire for God differs from that for men

Do not be surprised that I speak in this childlike way – seemingly, foolishly and inappropriately. I have certain reasons, and I think I have been moved for some time now to feel, think and speak in this way to some of my other special friends and now to you.

One of the reasons why I ask you to hide your heart's desire from God is this: I think your intention will come to his mind more clearly if you hide it than if you demonstrate it,

---

[1]A reference to Hebrews 12:20 and to Exodus 19:13: 'And if a beast shall touch the mount, it shall be stoned.'

whatever method you may choose. I believe, too, that concealment is better for you than open display and will much sooner fulfil your desire.

Another reason is this: by such a hidden demonstration I want to get you away from the rough, loud emotion of it all, and lead you to a purity and depth of spiritual experience. Then only will I finally be able to help you to tie that spiritual knot of burning love between you and your God in spiritual oneness and harmony of will.

You know well that God is Spirit, and whoever would be one with him must be so in truth and depth of spirit, far removed from any false bodily thing. It is true that everything is known to God and nothing may be hidden from him either in body or spirit. But since he is Spirit then that which is hidden in the depths of man's spirit is more clear and obvious to him than that which is mixed up with bodily things. For, by its nature, every physical thing is farther away from God than any spiritual thing. It would follow, then, that if our longing for God has any sort of physical element in it, (as for instance when we strain and stress ourselves emotionally and spiritually), then it becomes much further from God than it would be if there had been greater devotion, more sober eagerness, purity and spiritual depth.

You may now partly understand when I seem to talk about hiding your longing from God, as if I were advocating some childish game. Yet I don't say cloak it completely. That would be a fool's advice, to tell you to do something that quite plainly is impossible! At the same time, I am saying that you should do all you can to keep it hidden! Why is this? Because I want you to plunge into the depths of your spirit, to get right away from any mixture of crude physical showiness which would draw you further and further away from God. And I know very well that the more spiritual your soul becomes the less it desires physical sensation. Then it draws closer to God, pleases him more and is clearly more visible to him. Not that God's sight is ever dimmed, for God is ever without change, but the soul is more like God when it is pure in spirit, for God is spirit.

There is still another reason why you should do all you can to make sure that you do not display your intention to God. You and I, and others like us, are bound to see a spiritual thing in material terms. So if I had directed you to demonstrate your inner feelings of love to God, you would have done so in some physical way, either by gesture, voice, word, or some other primitive bodily action, as one would naturally do to another human being. In so doing your contemplation would have become impure. We demonstrate a thing to man in one way, but in quite another way to God.

48 Serving God in body and soul: distinguishing between good and evil comforts

I am not saying all this to prevent you from praying aloud whenever you are so moved, or to stop you from bursting out in your overflowing devotion of soul with 'Good Jesus!', 'Lovely Jesus!', 'Sweet Jesus!' No indeed! God forbid that you should so misunderstand my meaning. This is not what I mean at all. God forbid that I should part the body and the soul which God himself has joined. God wants to be served both by body and soul together, as is right, and he wants to give man his due heavenly reward both in body and soul.

As a foretaste of that reward God will at times inflame the physical body of his devout servant, and maybe not just once or twice but on a number of occasions, and as often and when he likes, with very wonderful sweetness and consolation. Not all of this will come from outside our bodies through the windows of our intellect, but from within, rising and springing from an overflowing and happy heart and true spiritual devotion. Such comfort and such sweetness is not suspect, and without saying more, I believe that he who enjoys it cannot regard it so.

But I strongly suggest that you do suspect all other comforts, sounds, gladness and sweetness that come suddenly from outside yourself, whose origin you do not know. They may be either good or evil, brought about by good or bad angels. However, they will not be evil if those wrong intellectual enquirings and improper emotional strainings are removed, in ways I have already suggested or in better ways that you yourself may know. Why is this? Surely it is because the cause of this comfort is the devout stirring of love which dwells within a pure spirit. It is directly created by the hand of Almighty God. So it must follow that it is far removed from fantasy or any kind of wrong opinion which a man may acquire in life.

Of the other comforts, sounds and sweetnesses, and how you can distinguish whether they are good or evil, I do not intend to tell you yet. This is not because I think it unnecessary, but because you can find it written about elsewhere. Even this you will find dealt with far better by someone else. But what of it? I shall still continue to meet your need. I shall not tire of satisfying that longing heart of yours, which you have shown me that you possess, first by your words and now in your actions.

But I will say this about those sounds and sweetnesses that come to us through the windows of our intellect, and which may be good or evil: continually practise this blind, devout, eager stirring of love that I've already spoken about, and I have no doubt that it will itself be able to tell you about all of this. If, when they first come, you are astonished – partly, if not wholly, because you are not used to them – this love within you will do one thing for you at least: it will bind your heart with such strong unity that you will never give them full credence unless you are absolutely sure of them. This assurance you will gain either through a wonderful inner approval by the Spirit of God or else from the outside advice of some discreet spiritual father.

49 Perfection is essentially good will: consolation is incidental

So I pray, incline eagerly towards this humble stirring of love within your heart and follow its leading. It will be your guide in this life and bring you to the bliss of heaven in the other. It is the substance of all good living. Without it no good work may be begun or ended. It is in essence a good will in harmony with God, and a kind of well-being and gladness that you experience in your will in everything God does.

Such an intention is the basis of all perfection. All sweetness and comfort, both physical and spiritual, however holy they may be, are by comparison incidental, and dependent upon this basic intention. 'Accidents' I call them, for they come and go. I refer to this life, of course. In heaven they will be inseparable, united with their substance as the body will be with the soul. Here on earth their substance is the good spiritual will. I know for certain that the man who has this perfect will (as perfect as is possible in this life) is as content not to have the consolations and sweetness as he is to have them, if God will it so.

50 Pure love: some experience consolation seldom, some often

In this way you will see that we should direct our every attention upon this humble movement of love in our will. We should react indifferently to other sweetness and comfort, physical or spiritual, however holy or pleasing (if I may be free to say so): If they come, welcome them, but do not

76

depend on them for they are weakening; it will take too much out of you to stay for any length of time in such sweet feelings and fears. You may keep on being drawn into loving God for the sake of having the feeling. You will know that this has happened if you start complaining when they are absent. If you do, your love is not yet pure and perfect. For pure perfect love, though it agrees that the body is sustained and comforted when such sweet feelings or fears are present, never grumbles when without them; it is just as pleased not to have those consolations, if it is God's will.

While in some people comfort and consolation is the norm, in others it is rare. It is entirely a matter of God's purpose and plan, according to the needs of each individual. Some people are so spiritually weak and sensitive that, if they did not receive God's comfort, they would find it impossible to bear the various temptations and tribulations which they have to suffer and endure in this life, and which come from their physical and spiritual foes. There are those who are so frail physically that they are unable to perform the penance needed for forgiveness. These people will be cleansed by our Lord, in his grace, with sweet emotions and tears. Then there are those, on the other hand, who are so strong in spirit that they glean all the comfort they require from within their own souls and have little need to be sustained with sweet emotions. They remain strong by offering up their reverent, humble, outreach of love and obedient will. Which of the two is holier or dearer to God is not for me to say. God alone knows.

51 Understanding spiritually not literally, particularly the words *in* and *up*

Attend to this unseen movement of love in your heart with all humility. Of course, I mean your spiritual heart which is your will, not your physical one. Be careful not to interpret physically what is meant spiritually. Much error is caused by the elaborate imaginings of inventive minds.

You can see an example of this in what I have already said about hiding your desire from God as best you can. If I had told you to show your desire for God, you would have understood it much more literally than you do now when I tell you to hide it. Now you clearly realise only too well that the thing deliberately hidden is that which lies deep in the depth of the spirit. So I think there is a great need to be aware of how to understand words intended spiritually: do not interpret them literally. In particular, we must take care with the words *in* and *up*. I strongly suspect these two words have been the cause of much error and wrong in would-be contemplatives. I know something of this from my own experience and hearsay, and would like to write on this a little here.

A newly converted young disciple in God's school thinks that, because of the short time he has given to penance and prayer (as advised by his counsellor), he is now able to engage in contemplation. He has heard and read about it and when he comes across statements like, 'A man shall gather all his powers within himself', or 'He shall climb above himself', he immediately misunderstands them. Because, of course, since the young disciple is still spiritually blind, his outlook is still of the world, and he views things literally from his natural state. Such people think that, because they find within themselves an innate desire for mystical things, they are therefore called by grace to such work.

If their spiritual counsellor disagrees that they are called to be contemplatives, they promptly find fault with him. They think (and probably say to others) that nobody really understands them! So, at once and all too quickly, such cheeky presumptuous intellects give up their humble prayerful and penitent lives, and embark upon what they think is the real spiritual work of the soul. And this, if the truth be told, is not physical or spiritual work. It is an unnatural perverseness, whose chief agent is the devil. It is the quickest way to death. Physically and spiritually it drives a man to madness. Indeed, it is madness, not wisdom. They, however, do not think so, for they mean to think of nothing but God in this work.

52 Errors in a presumptuous understanding of the word *in*

The madness I speak of comes about like this: these people read and hear what is said about stopping the 'exterior' working of their mind and working with their 'interior' mind. And, because they do not really understand what this interior work means, they do it wrongly. They turn their physical minds inwards to their bodies, which is against nature's course. They strain to see inner spiritual things with their natural eyes, and to hear within, with their outward ears, and to smell, taste, touch and so on.

They turn the natural order upside down. They burden their minds until eventually their brains are turned under the strain. Immediately then the devil has power to deceive them with false lights or sounds, sweet smells and wonderful tastes, glowings and burnings in their hearts, stomachs, backs, loins and limbs!

Yet they believe this fantasy is a real, peaceful contemplation of God, unhindered by proud empty thoughts. So it is in a way. They are so stuffed with their false selves that they are not disturbed by any further stupidity. Why? Because the devil who is tempting them now is the same devil who would be tempting them if they were on the right road. You know very well he won't hinder himself! He won't remove thoughts of God from them lest they become suspicious!

53 Consequences of false contemplation

The many expressions that are produced by those who counterfeit contemplation are weird and wonderful. They are more, much more, striking than those of God's true disciples, who are always most correct in their behaviour, physical or spiritual. But not so with these others! To look at them you would think they were mad! There they sit, staring (when their eyes are open) and leering as though they saw the devil. They should, indeed, watch out, for the fiend is not far at all!

Some of them fix their eyes as though they were sheep giddy from a bang on the head and about to die at any moment. Some hang their head on one side as if a worm were in their ear. Some squeak when they should speak, as if their spirit had left their bodies (the proper condition for a hypocrite!). Some cry and whine: they are so eager and hasty to speak their minds (heretics are like this, and all who uphold error with presumptuous and ingenious minds).

If you could see everything you would see such disorderly and unseemly behaviour! However, there are those clever enough to restrain themselves in front of others. But if they were to be seen in their homes, I reckon all would be revealed! I also believe that they would burst out at some point if anyone tried to contradict them. Yet they think that they act only out of love for God and to maintain truth! I honestly and truly believe that unless God stops them with a miracle of mercy, they will love God in this way until they end up going to the devil stark raving mad. I am not saying that the devil has got a servant who is so perfect that he has deceived and infected him with all the delusions outlined here (though it is possible that one, or maybe many, are infected with it all). However, I do say that though the devil may not totally possess a hypocrite or heretic here on earth, he is nevertheless responsible for some of the errors I have mentioned already – and those I will go on to mention, God willing.

Some people are so prone to these curious expressions and physical mannerisms that, when they listen to anything, they twist their heads strangely on one side, stick their chins in the air, and gape with their mouths, giving the impression that they hear with their mouths and not their ears! When they speak, some make the point by stabbing with their fingers, either on the other hand or on their breast, or even on the breast of the person they are addressing! Some cannot sit, stand or lie still without waggling their feet or else fidgeting with their hands. Some speak with great rowing movements of their arms as though they needed to swim the seas. Some are forever smiling and laughing at every other word they speak as though they were giddy girls or silly clowns who didn't know how to behave. Far better to have a modest expression, and to carry oneself calmly and soberly and with genuine happiness.

I am not saying that all these unseemly gestures are great sins in themselves nor that those who perform them are all great sinners. What I am saying is that if this uncontrolled behaviour takes hold of the man so that he cannot shed it, then that is a sure sign of pride, of an empty mind, of disordered behaviour and knowledge. In particular it indicates an unstable heart and restless mind that is unable to perform what this book urges. The only reason I have set out so many of these errors here is that a contemplative may test himself against them.

54 Contemplation makes one wise and attractive in body and soul

Anyone who engages in contemplation should find that it has a good effect on him in body and soul. It should make him more attractive to all who look at him. So much so that the world's ugliest person, who becomes a contemplative by

God's grace, finds that he is suddenly changed. Then every good man he sees is glad and happy to have his friendship because he is spiritually refreshed by it and helped to draw nearer to God.

Therefore seek to get this gift by grace. Whoever really has it will know how to control himself and his possessions. When necessary it will give him discernment into the characters and needs of others. To the astonishment of onlookers he will know just how to relate to each person he talks to, habitual sinners or not, without sinning himself. By God's grace he will be able to draw others to the same work that he practises.

From his face and his words should flow spiritual wisdom, full of fire and fruit, confident and free from falsehood, far removed from any pretence or the blurtings of hypocrites. For there are those who concentrate all their energy on studying how to speak powerfully, with many soft empty words and displays of devotion. They strive more towards looking holy to impress men than to be holy in the eyes of God and his angels. Why, these people get more hot and bothered over unorthodox ritual and indecent or bad language, than they do over a thousand proud thoughts or sickening sinful impulses, which they will have deliberately instigated or indulged in irresponsibly in the sight of God and his angels in heaven.

Ah, Lord God! Surely there is inner pride where there are so many outward humble squeaks. I readily grant that it is right and proper for those who are truly humble to express themselves by outward word and manner. But I can't agree that they should express themselves in squeaky high-pitched voices that are clearly at odds with their natural disposition. If someone is genuine, he speaks sincerely and his voice is in keeping with his spirit within. So if a man who is the naturally boisterous sort starts speaking with a pathetic, high-pitched squeak (unless, of course, he is ill or talking with God or in his confession!) then it is a very clear indication of hypocrisy. And this is true of both young and old alike.

What more shall I say of these poisonous errors? I honestly and truly believe that unless these people have the grace to leave off such hypocritical affectations, then, caught between their hidden pride and outward humility, these unfortunate souls will soon sink with sorrow.

55 Errors of those who fervently, injudiciously condemn sin

The fiend will deceive some people in a remarkable way: he will set them on fire to maintain the law of God and destroy sin in all others. He will never tempt them with anything that is openly evil. He makes them become like those busy ecclesiastics watching over every condition of our Christian life, as an abbot does over his monks. Just as if they had the cure for men's souls, they do not hesitate to reprove everyone for their faults. They think they dare not do otherwise, and they tell them their faults for God's sake. They say they have been moved to do so by their ardent love for others and by God's love in their hearts. They lie! It is the fire of hell flaring up in their minds and imagination.

What follows would seem to show that this is true. The devil is a spirit too, and no more has a body than has an angel. Yet when, by God's leave, he or an angel assumes a body in order to do something for a human being, he still retains something of his essential self; he is still recognisable. Scripture provides examples of this. In the Bible the essential errand of an angel, whenever he was sent in bodily form, was always revealed by his name or by something he did. It is the same with the fiend. When he appears in bodily form he betrays in some visible way what his servants are really like in spirit.

Let me take just one example of this. I understand from followers of necromancy, who claim to know how to call up wicked spirits and to whom the fiend has appeared in bodily shape, that, whatever likeness he assumes, he has never more than one large and flaring nostril, which he gladly turns up to let a man see through to his brain. This brain is nothing other than the fire of hell. The fiend can possess no other brain. And there is nothing he wants more than to turn a man's head to look. In so doing a man goes mad for ever. But an experienced practitioner of necromancy knows this well enough and can so arrange things that the man suffers no harm.

So, as I say, whenever the devil takes on bodily form he betrays in some visible way what his servants are like in their spirit. For he so inflames the imagination of his contemplatives with the fire of hell, that suddenly and roughly they shoot out their peculiar opinions, and, without waiting to see things clearly, will take upon themselves the task of condemning other men's faults. That division in a man's nose which separates the nostrils suggests that a man should have spiritual insight, and know how to distinguish good from evil, bad from worse, good from better, before he passes judgment on anything he has heard or seen around him. By a man's brain is spiritually understood the imagination; its rightful place and function is in the head.

56 Relying on human intellect and knowledge, instead of the Church, is deceptive

There are some who, though not deceived by the error just mentioned, do give up the doctrine and counsel of Holy Church because of their pride in their natural cleverness and intellect. These men and their supporters lean too much on their own learning. Because they were never grounded in this humble blind love and truly good living, they deserve to have a false experience, which has been counterfeited and produced by their spiritual enemy. Then finally they burst out into blasphemy of all the saints, sacraments, statutes and ordinances of Holy Church. Worldly, sophisticated men who think that they cannot reform their lives by the laws of the Church because they think the laws are too hard, too readily and too quickly incline to these heretics and staunchly support them. And it is all because they think they will be following a more comfortable way than that laid down by Holy Church.

Now I believe, in all honesty, that those who will not go the hard way to heaven will go the comfortable way to hell – as we shall all find out for ourselves. I believe that on the Last Day these heretics and their followers will be seen in their true light to be not only burdened and bent low with the great and horrible sins of the world and the flesh, which had been their secret sins, but also weighed down by the way in which they had, with bare-faced effrontery, upheld wrong. They will rightly be called disciples of Antichrist, for despite their apparent integrity in their public lives, they will be found filthy and debauched in private.

57   Misunderstanding the word *up* and the errors this brings

But no more of this for now. Let us move on to see how these presumptuous young disciples misunderstand the word *up*.

Should they hear or read that men ought to lift up their hearts to God, they immediately stare at the stars as if they wanted to get past the moon and listen out for angels singing from heaven. In their mental fantasies they penetrate the planets making a hole in the firmament to look through! They fashion a god to their own likeness, dressing him in rich clothes and setting him on a throne in a way that is more odd than any painting on this earth! These people would make angels take human shapes and stand them around playing different musical instruments, all much odder than we would ever see or hear on earth!

The devil will deceive some of these people most remarkably. He sends a kind of dew (they think it is angels' food) falling out of the air, as it were, gently into their mouths! So they have a habit of sitting open-mouthed as though they were catching flies! Now all this is simply pious fraud, for at such times their souls are totally empty of real devotion. Their hearts are full of pride and error because of their outrageous practices – so much so that the devil will deceive their senses with quaint sounds and flashing lights and wonderful smells. It is all false!

They, of course, don't see it. They think that they have for their example, in all this upward-looking business, St Martin, who by revelation saw God wearing his cloak among his angels. Or they point to St Stephen, who saw our Lord standing in heaven, or to other such saints. Or they refer to Christ himself, who was seen by his disciples ascending physically into heaven. So, they argue, we should look up. I readily grant that in our physical observances we should lift up our eyes and hands if the spirit so moves us. But I would say that the work of our spirit shall not be directed up or down, or to any side, as though it were a bodily thing. Our work is spiritual, not physical, and is not achieved in any physical fashion.

58 St Martin and St Stephen are not to be taken literally when understanding the word *up*

With regard to St Martin and St Stephen, although they saw these things with their physical eyes, they were revealed miraculously in order to demonstrate a spiritual truth. They knew perfectly well that St Martin's cloak was never really worn by Christ to keep out the cold, but was worn miraculously as a reminder to us all that we can be saved and united spiritually to the body of Christ. Whoever clothes a poor man out of love for God, whether physically or spiritually, may be quite sure that it is done spiritually to Christ. And they will be rewarded as if it had been actually done to Christ. He says this himself in the Gospel (Matt. 25:31–46). Yet, as though this wasn't enough, he subsequently confirmed it to St Martin by miracle in a special revelation.

All the revelations that men see here in human forms have spiritual meanings. And I believe if those who saw these things could have understood these things spiritually they would not have been given these physical visions. So let us strip off the outer husk of these matters and eat the sweet kernel of inner truth.

But how? Not like these heretics who have been likened to those mad folk whose custom it is to throw their beautiful cup against the wall when they have drunk from it. If we mean to make progress, we will not follow suit. We who feed on its fruit are not going to despise the tree, nor break the cup from which we have drunk. I call the tree and the cup visible miracles, like all those outward observances which help and do not hinder the Spirit. The fruit and the drink I would call the spiritual meaning behind these visible miracles, these outward observances like lifting up our eyes and hands towards heaven. If done by the Spirit's leading, well and good – otherwise it is hypocritical and false. If these are sincere and contain spiritual fruit, why despise them? For men will kiss the cup that holds the wine.

And what if our Lord, ascending physically to heaven, was literally seen by his mother and the disciples on the way up into the clouds? Are we then to stare upwards as we contemplate? Are we to look as if we hoped to see him sitting down in heaven, or standing, as Stephen saw him? Of course not!

Surely he did not reveal himself in human terms to St Stephen in order to teach us the spiritual truth that we must physically look up to heaven on the off-chance that we too might catch a glimpse of him standing, sitting or lying down! What his body is doing in heaven nobody knows! Nor do we need to know more than that his body is inseparably united with his soul; that his Manhood is in turn inseparably united with the Godhead. It is enough for us to know that – whether his body is sitting, standing or reclining – Christ is there in heaven doing what pleases him and is best for him. Should he reveal his postures to anyone, it is for a spiritual reason – not because he is actually taking that form in heaven.

This can be seen by an example. The word *stand* indicates a readiness to help. So it is often said between friends: 'Bear up, old chap; fight hard, don't give in too easily. I'll stand by you!' This does not mean just a physical standing by (though it could be if it were a cavalry charge!) but that, as a friend, he will be ready to help. For this same reason the Lord revealed himself to St Stephen in his martyrdom. It was not meant as an example for us to physically look up into heaven, but to say to St Stephen, who represents all who suffer for Christ out of love for him: 'Stephen, I open the vaults of heaven and let you see me physically so that you may also know that by the power of my Godhead I am standing by you spiritually, ready to help you. So stand firm in faith, bravely endure the dreadful hurt from those hard stones. Be sure that I shall crown you in heaven as a reward, and all others like you who suffer persecution for my sake!'

Now you can see how these outward displays were given for spiritual purposes.

If you are going to say of the ascension of our Lord that it must have had physical significance as well as spiritual, since it was a physical body that ascended and he is truly both God and Man, my answer is that our Lord had been dead and was clothed in an immortal body just as we shall be on Judgment Day. Then we shall be so different in our new body-soul natures that our bodies will be able to move in as many directions, and as swiftly, as we now move in thought. But right now you can only go to heaven spiritually. And it is so intensely spiritual that it cannot be physical at all, in any direction.

Ensure that all who mean to live the spiritual life, particularly that outlined in this book, clearly understand that any references to 'lift up', 'go in', 'moved by', are not intended as movements from one place to another and do not reach out in any physical sense! Even where the book talks of 'a rest', they must not think that it means staying permanently in one spot. Contemplative perfection is so finely spiritual that in understanding it correctly we would realise how poles apart it is from any physical movement or place.

It might more reasonably be called a sudden 'changing' rather than a movement. For time, place and body are all forgotten in contemplation. So be very careful not to interpret the physical ascension of Christ as an indication that you must strain your imagination physically upwards, as though your body were to rise above the moon. But then no one can do that except God, who said: 'No man can ascend to heaven but he that came down from heaven, and became man for the love of men' (John 3:13).

Even if it were possible, which it isn't, it would only be for richer spiritual activity, given solely by the power of the spirit, devoid of all physical strain and stress on the imagination. So leave such wrong alone; heaven cannot come this way.

60 The way to heaven is by desire, not on foot

It may well be that you are asking: 'How do you arrive at these conclusions?' You think you have evidence that heaven is up above, for Christ physically ascended upward, and later he sent the promised Holy Spirit (unseen by any disciple) from above. And, of course, we believe this. So, you wonder, why should you not, literally, direct your mind upward when you pray?

Let me answer as best I can. Since it had to be that Christ should ascend physically and send the Holy Spirit in tangible form, it was more appropriate that it should be from above rather than from below, the front, the back or anywhere else. There was no need for Christ to go in any direction (the way is so near) except that it suited God's purpose. In spiritual terms, heaven is as near whether up, down, before, behind, this side or that! Anyone really wanting to be in heaven is there immediately in the spirit. We run there by the highest and quickest way – by our desires, not our feet! So St Paul says that although our bodies are here on earth we nevertheless live in heaven (Phil. 3:20). He means that our love and spiritual lives are in heaven and that this is our true life. Surely it is as true to say that a soul is where the object of his love is, as to say that it is in its body, which depends upon it and to which it gives life. So, if we are to be in heaven spiritually, we do not have to strain our spirits in any physical direction whatever!

Yet, when and if the spirit dictates, there is a need for us to lift up our physical eyes and hands to the starry heavens above. For the body is subject to the things of the spirit and is controlled by it, not the other way round.

Our Lord's ascension is an example of this. When the appointed time came for him to return to his Father in the body of his Manhood (he never ceased nor could ever cease to be God), then – because God is Spirit – the body of his Manhood, with all God's innate power, followed into the unity of one Person. The visible display of this took the most suitable form: upwards.

This subjection of the body to the spirit may, in a way, be experienced by those seeking to put this book's teaching into practice. When a soul is determined to engage in this work, then, without realising it, the body, once bent and drooped, suddenly lifts up, straightened out by the spirit, and shows outwardly what has happened inwardly by the spirit. All just how it should be!

And because it is so right, man, who of all creatures has the most suitable bodily form, is not made crooked, facing down like the other animals, but upright, facing heavenwards. This is because the physical body should reflect the likeness of the spiritual soul, which should be spiritually upright and not bent down. Note that I said 'spiritually upright' and not 'physically': how can a soul be strained upright physically when, by its nature, it is without a body? It cannot be done.

So take care, then, not to interpret physically what is intended spiritually, even though it is expressed in physical terms, like 'up, down, in, out, behind, before, this side, that side'. Even the most spiritual thing of all, if it were to be spoken of (and speech is an action of the tongue, which is part of the body) must necessarily be spoken of in physical words.

But what of it? Should it then be interpreted physically? No, not at all, but rather spiritually.

62 How to understand spiritual working

So, in order that you may more easily understand when words spoken by the tongue are meant to be taken spiritually, I will explain to you the spiritual significance of some of these words when they are used in connection with the spiritual life. Then you will know for certain when the spiritual work is inferior to you and exterior, when it is interior and on your level, as it were, and when it is superior to you, just below God himself.

Everything physical is external to your soul and inferior to it in the natural order of things – sun, moon, and stars may all be above your physical body but they are beneath your soul.

Although angels are more beautiful and strong in grace and virtue and superior in purity to human souls, they are nevertheless on the same level in the natural order.

Your soul has within itself, in the natural order, these three principal faculties: mind (which includes memory), reason, and will; and two minor ones: imagination and sensuality.

In the natural order of things there is nothing higher than yourself except God alone.

Whenever you come across the word *yourself* in spiritual writings, it is your soul that is meant, and not your body. The work and quality of your soul is determined by the object upon which your soul's powers are directed.

63 Faculties of the soul: the mind embraces all others

The mind has such a power in itself that, generally speaking, it does not work on its own. The reason, will, imagination and sensuality are the faculties that work with, and are held and embraced by, the mind. Only in this collective sense can the mind be said to work.

Some of the spiritual faculties I call major, some minor – not because it is possible to divide the soul into parts, but because its operations can be analysed: those that are major are all spiritual activities, and those that are minor are all material activities.

The two major faculties, reason and will, work entirely on their own in all spiritual matters, unaided by the minor faculties. Imagination and sensuality, however, work in all forms of animal and physical life, irrespective of reason or will. They are physical activities working with the physical senses. But by these two alone, unaided by reason and will, a soul can never know the moral world and right standards of the natural world, nor could it see the reason for its existence or its actions.

So we call reason and will major faculties, for they work purely in spirit, independent of material things. The imagination and sensuality are minor attributes because they work in the body with its five senses. Mind is called a major faculty because spiritually it embraces within itself not only all the other faculties but also those things through which they work. Consider the evidence.

64 Sin affects reason and will

Reason is the faculty by which we distinguish evil from good, bad from worse, good from better, worse from worst, and better from best. Before man's sin, reason would have done this in the light of nature. But now it is so blinded by original sin that it cannot do this unless it is illumined by grace. Both reason itself and the means through which it works are held and stored in the mind.

Will is the faculty through which we choose good after it has been discerned by reason. Through it we love God, desire him and finally dwell in him with complete satisfaction and consent. Before man sinned, his will could not go wrong in its choice, its love, or in anything it did because, by its nature, it understood each thing clearly. But it is unable to do so now unless it is anointed with grace. Often now, because of the infection of original sin, it assesses a thing good when it has only a veneer of good, and is in reality bad. Both the will and the thing willed are held within the mind.

65 Sin affects the imagination and its obedience to reason

Imagination is the faculty by which we can picture anything absent or present. Both it and the means by which it works are contained in the mind. Before man sinned, the imagination was so obedient to its master, reason, that it never pictured anything that was perverted, or fantasised in any way physically or spiritually. Now, this is not so. If it is not restrained by reason in the light of grace, it will endlessly continue to suggest – in either the sleeping or waking states – various perverted ideas of the world. Or it will hallucinate, which is only a spiritual idea seen in material terms or the other way round. This is always counterfeit and false, the next thing to error.

This disobedience of the imagination is seen clearly in the prayers of those newly converted to the life of devotion. Until the time when their imagination is largely controlled by the light of grace in their reason (which happens after continual meditation on spiritual things such as their own wretchedness, the passion and kindness of our Lord, and so on), they cannot dispel the amazing range of thought, hallucinations and images which are projected and imprinted on their minds by their fertile imagination. All this disobedience is the result of original sin.

66 Sin affects sensuality and its obedience to will

Sensuality is the faculty of our soul which affects and controls all our physical actions. Through it we know and feel the physical world, whether pleasant or unpleasant. It has two functions: one which looks after our physical needs and one which serves the physical appetites. It is the same faculty which grumbles when the body lacks something it essentially requires, and yet, when the need is met, will urge it to take more than it needs in order to maintain and further its desires. If its likes are not met it grumbles, and is thoroughly delighted when it is satisfied. It grumbles in the presence of what it dislikes and is highly pleased when it is removed. This faculty and the means through which it works are contained in the mind.

Before man sinned, sensuality was obedient to its master, the will. It never led into perverted or pretended physical pleasure or pain brought into the mind by the devil. But this is not so now. Sensuality must be ruled by will, through grace, so that in humility it readily suffers the full measure of the consequences of original sin (which it feels in the absence of its wanton pleasure and has to be content with those annoying things that are good for it!). It must control its strong desires: both its wanton pleasure, and also its greedy delight when the annoying things (really beneficial for it) are removed! Unless it can do these things, it will wallow like a pig in the mire, wretched and wild in the filth of worldly pleasure, until its whole life becomes animal and physical rather than human and spiritual.

67 Deception in spiritual understanding, and a soul made 'a god' through grace

My spiritual friend, you see to what base levels we have fallen through sin. No wonder we are totally and easily deceived when we try to understand spiritual words and actions, particularly when we do not yet know the faculties of our soul and how they work.

Whenever the mind is occupied with any physical thing, however honourable, you are still 'beneath' the mind and 'outside' the soul. And whenever you feel your mind occupied by the subtleties of the soul's faculties and its spiritual workings (such as vices or virtues, in you or in others like you) so that you may know yourself better and become more perfect, then you will be 'within' yourself and level with yourself. But when you feel your mind engaged with God alone (as this book will testify) and not in any other physical or spiritual activity, then you can be said to be 'above' yourself, and 'beneath' God himself.

Indeed, you are above yourself because, by grace, you have attained what you could never naturally achieve. That is, you have become one with God, united in spirit, love and harmony of will. You are, however, beneath God, for although at this time you are in a way one spirit with him (so that you, or anyone else who perfectly contemplates, may truly be called 'a god' in this unity, as the Bible says (John 10:34), you are nevertheless beneath God. For God exists by his nature without beginning, but you were once nothing at all. When, later, by his power and love, you were made something, by a

96

deliberate act of your will you made yourself less than nothing. It is entirely by God's undeserved mercy and grace that you are made a god, inseparably united to him in spirit both now and in the bliss of heaven, world without end! So although, by grace, you are wholly one with God, yet by nature you are far beneath him.

My spiritual friend, now perhaps you see a little of how a man who does not understand his faculties, what they are or how they work, may very easily be deceived by words intended spiritually. And you may also understand something of the reason why I dare not urge you plainly to show your longing to God, but rather I suggest you do your best to hide it as in a child's game. I do this because I really fear that you may understand physically things which are intended spiritually.

68 Nowhere physically is everywhere spiritually

Whereas another man might tell you to collect all your powers and thoughts within yourself and worship God there, and he would be speaking perfectly correctly, yet I do not care to do this in case you are misled into a wrong physical interpretation of these words. But what I will say is this: see that you do not in any way withdraw into yourself. To be brief, I do not want you to be outside, above, behind or beside yourself either!

So you say, 'Well then, where am I to be? Nowhere according to you!' That is it exactly; that is just where I want you to be. The reason is that nowhere physically is everywhere spiritually. Make it your business to see that your spirit is fixed on no physical thing. Then you will find that wherever the object of your mind lies, there you are in spirit, just as surely as your body is where you are bodily!

And though your natural mind can now find 'nothing' to feed on, for it thinks it is nothing that you do, continue to do nothing and do so for the love of God. Do not stop but continue working hard on that nothing, with vigilance and longing, willing yourself to have God, whom no man can know. For I can truly tell you that I would rather be nowhere physically, wrestling with that unknown nothing, than be some great lord who could go everywhere, whenever he liked and enjoy everything, as though it were all his.

Let go this 'everywhere' and this 'everything'; exchange it for 'nowhere' and 'nothing'. Do not worry if you cannot understand this nothing, for that's why I love it so. It is in itself so worthy a thing that no thinking about it will do it justice. This nothing may be felt more than it can be seen. To those who have only just begun to look for it, it is completely dark and hidden. Yet, to be more accurate, it is an overwhelming spiritual light that blinds the soul who is experiencing it, rather than an actual darkness or the lack of physical light. Who then calls it 'nothing'? Surely that is the outer man speaking, not the inner self. The inner man calls it 'All'. For through it he is taught the secret of all things, physical and spiritual, without special reference to any one thing on its own.

69 An altered outlook by spiritual experience of nothing in its nowhere

A man's outlook is wonderfully changed when he has this spiritual experience of nothing in its nowhere. When the soul first looks upon it he finds his past sins, spiritual and physical, which he has committed since birth, painted secretly and darkly there. They meet his eyes at every turn until – at last after much labour, heartfelt sighs and bitter tears – he rids himself of them.

Sometimes, as he is engaged in this hard work, he thinks he might well be looking at hell; he feels such despair and it seems so impossible that perfection and peace could ever be attained out of all that pain. Many people come as far as this on their inward pilgrimage but, because the suffering is so great and they get no comfort, they return to their worldly pursuits. They look for physical and external comfort to compensate for the missing spiritual comfort (as yet undeserved) which they would have gained had they persevered.

For it is the man that abides, who perseveres, who feels comfort and has hope of gaining perfection. He begins to feel and see that many of his past sins are, by grace, mostly rubbed away. Though he still suffers, he believes it will end one day, for it decreases all the time. So now he calls it purgatory, rather than hell. Sometimes he can find no special sin written there, though he still thinks of sin in terms of 'a lump' which he knows is himself and does not analyse. Then it may be called the root and painful result of original sin. At times he believes his state to be paradise or heaven because he finds many wonderful, varied delights, comforts, joys and blessed virtues. Sometimes he believes it is God, because of the peace and rest he discovers.

Yet, think what he will, he will always find it to be a cloud of unknowing between him and his God.

70 Cessation of both natural and spiritual understanding

Work hard and fast at this 'nothing' and this 'nowhere'[1] and put aside your outward physical ways of knowing and doing things, for I can tell you truly that this work cannot be understood in this way.

[1]'Nothing' and 'nowhere' are the divine cloud of unknowing.

Your eyes tell you what it is you are seeing – whether it is long, broad, small, big, round or square, near or far and what colour it is. Your ears help you understand by the sound it makes, your nose by the smell; your taste tells you whether it is sweet, sour, salty, fresh, bitter or pleasant; your touch whether it is hot, cold, hard, soft, blunt or sharp.

But God and spiritual things do not possess any of these qualities. So leave all outer knowledge gained through the senses. Do not work with them at all, either objectively or subjectively. For all who intend to become contemplatives and think that they will hear, see, smell, taste or feel spiritual things externally or internally, are seriously mistaken: this would be to work against the natural course of things.

For the senses acquire knowledge of the external physical world, but they do not give us spiritual understanding. However, when we recognise their limitations, we may gain spiritual knowledge. For example, when we read or hear certain things which we fail to understand through our natural faculties, then we may be sure that they are not physical but spiritual.

Similarly, it occurs in spiritual matters, when within our hearts we strive to know God himself. No matter how well versed a man is in spiritual knowledge and no matter how well he understands the creation, he can never come to know an uncreated spiritual thing – which is God himself. But, by recognising the reason why his understanding is limited, he may discern that which is God. This is why St Dionysius said: 'The most Godlike knowledge of God is that which is known by unknowing.' Indeed, anyone reading Dionysius's work will see that he confirms all that I have said from start to finish. Otherwise I would not care about quoting him or any other teacher. There was a time when it was a sign of humility to support one's own original thoughts and words by citing scripture and learned quotations. Today it has become a way of parading one's cleverness and erudition. You do not need this and so I am not doing it. For 'whoever has ears, let him hear' and anyone moved to believe, let him believe; there is no other way.

71 Perfection felt in ecstasy, also at will

There are some who think that contemplation is so difficult and frightening that they say it cannot be accomplished without a great deal of hard work first. Further, it can only occur occasionally and then only in a time of complete ecstasy. To this I will answer as well as I can: it entirely depends upon God's will and pleasure, coupled with the person's ability to receive this grace and working of the Spirit in contemplation.

There will be some who cannot attain this state without a long hard struggle beforehand. They may then have rare experiences of its fullness in response to a special call of our Lord: this we would call 'ecstatic'.

There are others who, by grace, are so sensitive spiritually and so at home with God in this grace of contemplation that they may have it when and where they like – in the midst of everyday actions whether walking, sitting, standing or kneeling. At these times they are in complete control of their faculties, both physical and spiritual, and can use them if they wish; admittedly not without some difficulty but not with great difficulty.

We can see the first kind of experience illustrated in Moses and the second in Aaron, the temple priest. The grace of contemplation is prefigured in the old law by the Ark of the Covenant, and the contemplatives by those who looked after the Ark, as the story shows. Both this grace and this work of contemplation can be likened to that Ark: just as the Ark contained all the jewels and relics of the temple, so this little love on this cloud of unknowing holds within itself all the virtues of a man's soul, which is the spiritual temple of God.

Before Moses could see the Ark and learn how it was to be made, he had to climb with great effort to the top of the mountain (Exod. 24:15–18). There he stayed and worked in a cloud for six days. On the seventh day our Lord condescended to show him how to make the Ark. Moses's long and strenuous efforts and his delayed vision stand for those who cannot come to such heights of spiritual perfection without first toiling hard – and even then the full experience comes only occasionally and is entirely at God's pleasure.

Moses could only see on rare occasions and then after much hard work. Aaron, on the other hand, because of his office as priest, could go into the temple behind the veil when he liked. Aaron stands for all those just mentioned, who by their spiritual wisdom and by grace may achieve perfect contemplation when they like.

72 Contemplatives do not judge each other

So you can see by all this that a man who has to work hard to attain perfect contemplation (and then but seldom) may be quite wrong to judge others by his own experience and to believe that this way is the only possible way. Similarly, the man who can achieve it whenever he likes would be quite wrong to judge others by his own standards, thinking he has the only way. Should such judgments be allowed? Certainly not! A man must not be allowed to think like that. It may well be that the first type of contemplative may become like the second. It was true of Moses: first he could only see the Ark rarely, in a limited way, and then only after the great effort of climbing the mountain. But later Moses had the vision as often as he liked in the valley down from the mountain.

The three men that had the most to do with the Ark of the Old Testament were Moses, Bezaleel and Aaron. On the mountain Moses got the instructions for its design; Bezaleel constructed it in the valley according to the revealed pattern, and Aaron kept it in the temple to handle and see as often as he liked.

In these three men we have varying examples of the ways in which the grace of contemplation can benefit us. Sometimes the benefit is solely by grace: then we are like Moses, who struggled up the mountain and had the vision but seldom and only when God chose to grant it and not as a reward for his labour. Sometimes the benefit is the result of our spiritual skill as well as God's grace: then we are like Bezaleel, who was not able to see the Ark before he had made it by his own efforts, but was, however, enabled to do so by the pattern revealed. Then sometimes we may also benefit by other men's teaching and then are like Aaron, who was in charge of the Ark fashioned by Bezaleel. It was his custom to handle and see the Ark and he could do so whenever he pleased.

My spiritual friend, though I speak childishly and out of ignorance, wretched sinner that I am, and though unfit to teach anyone, I bear the office of Bezaleel, making and placing into your hands, as it were, the spiritual Ark. You will have to work harder and better than I if you would be like Aaron: work at it constantly for your own sake and mine. Do this, I beg you, for the love of Almighty God. And since we are both called by God to this work of contemplation, I strongly urge you, for the love of God, to make up on your part what is lacking in mine.

If you think that this kind of contemplative work does not suit your temperament, either physically or spiritually, then you may leave it alone. Take another spiritual path under sound advice and without any blame. I must then ask you to excuse me, for it was my genuine intention to help you out of my limited knowledge. So read this book over two or three times, the more often the better, and you will understand it better. Perhaps some sentence that was too difficult on first or second reading will soon become easy.

Indeed, it seems impossible to understand how any would-be contemplative could read, speak or hear of this work without feeling a real concern for its outcome. So, if you think it is doing you good, give God heartfelt thanks and, for the love of God, pray for me.

Now act on it! And I beg you for the love of God, do not let anyone see this book unless, in your opinion, he is able to benefit from it (as I outlined earlier). If any such person does see it, I beg you to insist that he give himself plenty of time to go through it. For there may be some matter in the beginning or the middle which is left in the air and not fully explained in its context. But if it is not dealt with there it will be soon after or at the end. If anyone sees these matters only partially, he may easily go wrong; so I beg you to do as I say. If you think you need further information on any particular aspect, let me know what it is and your own opinion of it and I will try my best to put this right.[1]

But I do not want the idle-chatterers, flatterers, fault-finders, gossips, tell-tales and grumblers of every kind to see this book. I never intended to write it for them. So I would prefer that they did not read it, nor the learned (and un-learned) people who are merely curious – even if they may be

[1]The disciple accepted this offer and so we have the author's reply in the *Epistle of Privy Counsel.*

good men, judged from an active standpoint. All this will mean nothing to them.

75 Signs to prove whether one is called to contemplation or not

Not everyone who reads this book is called by God to the contemplative life. They may well read it or hear about it and think what a good and pleasant thing it is and may even feel pleasant sensations when it is read! But this urge might well be stirred within them out of a naturally curious mind rather than from a call of grace.

But if they want to test the origin of their urge they may, if they like, do so in the following way. In the first place let them see if they have done everything they can to prepare for it by cleansing their conscience according to the law of Holy Church and the advice of their spiritual counsellor. So far so good. If they seek further assurance, then let them see if this urge constantly and habitually claims their attention more than other spiritual work. And if they come to believe that their conscience will not really approve anything they do, spiritual or physical, unless this secret little love which is fixed on the cloud of unknowing is the mainspring of their spiritual work, then it is a sign that God is calling them to this work; otherwise not.

I am not saying that this urge goes on for ever, continually filling the thoughts of those called to contemplation. This is not so. The actual urge is often withdrawn from the contemplative novice for many reasons. Sometimes it is because he may be taking it for granted too much, thinking that it generally lies in his own power to have it when and as often as he likes. This is nothing but pride. Whenever the feeling of grace is withdrawn, pride is always the cause; perhaps not actual pride but potential pride, which would have arisen had not the feeling been withdrawn.

Because of this there are some silly young people who think that God is their enemy, when really he is their best friend. Sometimes it is withdrawn because of their carelessness. When this is the case, they experience a deep bitterness which eats into them. Sometimes our Lord deliberately delays the feeling of grace, because in so doing he wishes to make it grow and be more treasured, like a precious thing lost and rediscovered. One of the surest and most important ways by which a soul may know if he is called to contemplation (after such a period of long inability to contemplate) is that it returns suddenly, independently of him, and he has a burning and deep passion to do this work as never before. Often, I think, his joy at its recovery is far greater than his distress at its loss! If this is the case, then it is unmistakably a true sign that he has been called by God to become a contemplative, irrespective of his former or present state.

For it is not what you are or have been that God looks upon with merciful eyes, but what you long to be. St Gregory says that 'all holy desires grow by delays; if they fade by these delays they were never holy desires.' If a man feels increasingly less joy at new discoveries and at the upsurge of his old, deliberate, desire for good, then those passions were never holy. St Augustine speaks of these holy desires saying that 'the life of a good Christian consists of nothing else but holy desire.'

Farewell, spiritual friend, with God's blessing upon you, and mine also! I pray that Almighty God grant you true peace, sound counsel and his own spiritual comfort with abundant grace. May it stay with you, and all who love God here on earth, for ever! Amen.

Short Bibliography

Hodgson, Dr Phyllis, *The Cloud of Unknowing* (Oxford University Press, 1944)

McCann, Abbot Justin, *The Cloud of Unknowing and Other Treatises*, with a commentary on the text by Father Augustine Baker (Burns Oates, 1924, revised ed. 1952)

Knowles, Dom D., *The English Mystics* (London, 1927)

Underhill, E., *The Cloud of Unknowing* (London, 1912)

Brother Lawrence

THE PRACTICE OF THE PRESENCE OF GOD

The conversation, letters, ways and spiritual principles of Brother Lawrence, the seventeenth century French monk who in his monastery kitchen discovered an overwhelming delight in God's presence.

This translation by Professor Blaiklock of the enduring spiritual classic includes a substantial introduction, setting Brother Lawrence in the context of his time and its thinking.

E. M. Blaiklock

THE CONFESSIONS OF
ST AUGUSTINE

Augustine towered as a Christian leader in his own age and probably made a greater contribution to the Church and Christian understanding than anyone else outside the New Testament.

The Confessions are his most famous book and have become a classic of all time. They reveal an unmistakable individual in the joys and agonies of life lived to the full in search of truth. But above all they are Augustine's shining testimony to the grace of God.